I0559216

Special Agent

My work as a Special Agent within the Department of
Homeland Security, Immigration and Customs
Enforcement, and my career persisted until my
retirement.

By

Donald R. Smith

Preface

In my first book, I Never Saw It Coming, I outlined my career, explaining how I began as a small-town police officer and progressed to a position as a Special Agent with the federal government. I also discussed how I would relocate my family across the country with me, living in nine different cities while taking on new law enforcement roles.

My second publication, I Was a Police Officer, reflects my experiences as a police officer in both Amite City and the Baton Rouge City police. I described my work as a police officer before transitioning into federal law enforcement service. I discussed my experiences working in uniform patrol, as a detective, a narcotics agent, a homicide detective, and in the motorcycle division.

In my third publication, U.S. Immigration Through My Eyes, I detailed my responsibilities as a U.S. Border Patrol Agent along the southern border, my duties within the U.S. Immigration Service, and my roles as a Supervisory Immigration Inspector and Area Port Director for the U.S. Virgin Islands.

This is my fourth book, and it begins with my appointment as a Supervisory Special Agent for U.S. Immigration in the New Orleans District Office. I was appointed to oversee the Criminal Alien Program and also explained the name change we underwent on March 1, 2003.

I transferred from New Orleans to U.S. Immigration and Customs Enforcement (ICE) Headquarters as the Section Chief for the Asset Forfeiture Unit (AFU). I oversaw 26 investigative field offices involving criminal forfeiture.

At ICE headquarters, I transitioned from the AFU to the Office of Professional Responsibility (OPR), which serves as the Internal Affairs Unit within the Department of Homeland Security.

I happily returned home to New Orleans and spent the final chapter of my career at the OPR New Orleans field office. After 46 years in law enforcement, I retired joyfully, bringing to a close a fulfilling and dedicated career.

Please note that the information in this book is based on my memories and the daily journals I kept. It combines my opinions and personal experiences, which allow me to write this book.

So, if you haven't already, please pick up my three previous books to gain a more transparent and precise understanding of my career, from my early years to my retirement.

Dedication

My wife, Linda,

Reflecting on my forty-six years in law enforcement, one constant has been your unwavering support, love, and partnership. This isn't just gratitude; it's a heartfelt tribute to the strength and grace you've brought into my life, standing with me through every challenge, victory, and trial along this long journey.

The early days were full of energy and the uncertainty that comes with starting something new. Fresh out of the academy, with my badge still shining brightly, I was full of ambition but also very aware of the risks and sacrifices that lay ahead. It was your kind encouragement and your unwavering belief in my calling that gave me the confidence to face each day. You understood, even then, how demanding the hours could be and how unpredictable the job was, and your support never wavered.

Law enforcement is a challenging field that requires courage, composure under pressure, and empathy during times of tragedy. Throughout difficult nights and harsh times, you were there. I recall the long shifts into the early hours, the phone calls with bad news, and times when I felt overwhelmed. In those moments, your reassurance, gentle words, steady support, and steadfast belief helped me stay focused on what truly counts.

You carried the worries that come with loving someone in this line of work. The silent prayers, sleepless nights, and the strength needed to face each day with hope did not go unnoticed. Your courage was as strong as mine, and I am endlessly thankful for your resilience.

Despite the challenges, there were moments of happiness, promotions, awards, solved cases, and new friendships. Every milestone felt more meaningful because I shared it with you. You celebrated my successes as if they were yours, and your pride elevated me beyond any award or ceremony.

You made our home a sanctuary, a place where I could shed the weight of the badge and be myself. The laughter around our dinner table, the warmth of our shared evenings, and the traditions you kept alive for our family became the true rewards of the life we built together.

There were sacrifices, too, birthdays missed, holidays spent on duty, moments in our son, Jacob's, life that I could not be present for. Through it all, you never complained. Your patience, understanding, and willingness to shoulder extra responsibilities at home have allowed me to serve with honor. You kept our family strong and thriving, even when my work kept me away.

So much of what I accomplished over these forty-six years came not from my own determination alone, but from your quiet strength and steadfast support. You were the foundation upon which my career was built, and you continue to be the heart of my life.

My career in law enforcement may have defined me to many, but you defined my journey. Your love sustained me, inspired me, and gave purpose to my work. I am proud of the years I served, but most proud to have shared them with you.

Our story is not only about endurance, but about partnership. It is a testament to the power of love, the resilience of the human spirit, and the extraordinary bond we share.

As all my suits and ties are folded away and the badge is laid to rest, I look forward to the days ahead, filled with new memories, new adventures, and the ongoing joy of your companionship.

Thank you for your patience, your warmth, and your faith in me. Thank you for every sacrifice, every smile, every word of encouragement, and every moment of understanding. You have been my steadfast partner and the greatest blessing of my life.

With all my heart, I dedicate this book, this journey, and every success along the way to you.

Table of Contents

Introduction

Before you get started reading this book, if you haven't already, please read my previous books, "I Never Saw It Coming," "I Was A Police Officer," and "U.S. Immigration Through My Eyes." These three books detail my journey into law enforcement, my experiences as a police officer, and the various positions I held throughout the federal government. They will guide you to this book, and you will understand things better.

While working as the Area Port Director in the U.S. Virgin Islands, specifically on St. Thomas, I was selected to fill the vacancy in New Orleans as a Supervisory Special Agent for U.S. Immigration.

On May 30, 2002, I received official orders transferring me from the US Virgin Islands to the Immigration and Naturalization Service (INS) Investigations in New Orleans, Louisiana. I was assigned to the New Orleans District Office.

Transferring to New Orleans felt like going back home for me, in a way. I was originally from Amite, which is on the North Shore of Tangipahoa Parish. When I started working for the U.S. Border Patrol, I was living in Amite. Now I've come full circle and returned home.

It was a lengthy journey, involving various positions and

multiple locations, all while bringing my family along with me.

Linda talks today about her knowledge of law enforcement, which she gained by hanging around with me. She will tell you that if it doesn't look right, then it probably isn't. When she goes to grocery stores or anywhere alone, she constantly watches her surroundings for anything out of the ordinary. She says that I taught her well, but the bottom line is, you have to want to learn. And she did.

I worked in OPR New Orleans until December 2022, when I decided to retire. After forty-six years in law enforcement, it was the closing of a chapter in my life. It's humbling to look back on the day I first donned the uniform. The world was different then, policies shifted with the political wind, technology lagged behind the imaginations of today, and our role was still being defined in the national consciousness.

What I will carry with me most vividly are the stories: the people whose paths crossed mine, sometimes for a moment, sometimes for years.

Forty-six years have taught me more than any manual or policy ever could. I have learned the value of listening before acting, recognizing that every situation holds layers unseen at first glance. Patience, humility, and courage are the qualities that have served me best, especially in the face of uncertainty.

Forty-six years ago, I answered a call to serve. Now, I answer a call to reflect and to begin again. I am proud of the career I have built, the colleagues I have worked alongside, and the difference we have made together. I leave knowing that the legacy of an agent is not in awards or accolades, but in the quiet moments of integrity and the lives changed for the better.

Chapter 1

Supervisory Special Agent

I have had a long and distinguished career in law enforcement. I began my career as a small-town police officer with the Amite Police Department (APD) in Amite, LA, and later joined the Baton Rouge Police Department (BRPD) in Baton Rouge, LA. After spending over nine years with the BRPD, I became a U.S. Border Patrol Agent on the southern border in Marfa, Texas. Later, I held various positions, including Immigration Inspector, Examiner, and Supervisory positions, as well as served as Area Port Director for the U.S. Virgin Islands and Supervisory Special Agent.

My prior books explain in detail how I reached this point in my career. I Never Saw It Coming, I Was A Police Officer, and U.S. Immigration Through My Eyes, all explain my journey and will bring you right up to this point.

On May 30, 2002, I received my official orders transferring me from the U.S. Virgin Islands, where I served as Area Port Director for the U.S. Immigration and Naturalization Service (INS), to the Immigration Investigations, New Orleans, Louisiana District Office, as a Supervisory Special Agent.

At the time, I had been working for the federal government

for 14 years. This was another government-funded move for me, and my wife, Linda, no longer had to worry about the school systems for our son, Jacob. Although I was working out of the New Orleans field office, we would live in our hometown of Amite.

Amite was our home, and where I started my career with the federal government in May 1988. We lived in a house on Ellis Road when I began, and now we are returning home after all these years. This meant Linda didn't have to learn where the grocery stores were, as she already knew where everything was located in Amite. Additionally, Linda's mother, Dorothy "D-Dot" Alford, also resided in Amite.

The feeling I had when I got back home was hard to put into words. It was emotional because, for years, I prayed to return home and not die in some city where I was working at the time. I always worried that something might happen to me, leaving Linda alone to handle everything.

My relocation from the U.S. Virgin Islands to New Orleans was the most seamless and straightforward of all our government moves. Everything proceeded without issue, and we faced no major problems. It took just a few weeks for me to get my official travel orders, and all government funds were readily available.

First day on duty

My first day reporting to New Orleans was on July 1, 2002, and I started by meeting with the District Director of Investigations. He kindly explained how the New Orleans office operated, and then he assigned me to oversee a team of special agents (SA) in the Criminal Alien Program (CAP).

I spent the day meeting with my team members, and we went out for lunch to get better acquainted with each other. They kindly shared their insights on current issues in the unit and the cases they're handling, providing an excellent opportunity to connect and learn more about each other.

Later, I connected with supervisors from various divisions to introduce myself and gain an understanding of their units and roles.

My duties as a Supervisory Special Agent

As a Supervisor, I managed a team of Special Agents (Criminal Investigators) and technical support staff assigned to the CAP. I enjoyed coordinating the growth and development of our unit, as well as overseeing daily operations.

I offered helpful recommendations and proactively worked to improve our unit's efficiency and productivity. I also developed a long-term plan to prepare for future changes and enhance the program's overall performance, ultimately benefiting both the team and staff.

I thoroughly reviewed and approved the distribution of leads, complaints, and allegations received from multiple sources, as well as investigative trends within cases.

My primary goal was to contribute to the development of thorough investigative plans and participate in conducting investigations, as well as managing complex cases.

I received extensive training in enforcement and federal law. I had to study and review case laws, agency regulations, and legal opinions to guide my unit in conducting investigations properly.

I established and maintained liaison contacts across all sectors of law enforcement and the intelligence community, as this was essential for gathering information about potential criminal violations. This process involved monthly meetings with other federal agencies and local law enforcement.

To supervise a group of special agents was to stand at the intersection of art and science. It required an unwavering commitment to the mission, a deep respect for the individuals entrusted to my command, and a relentless drive for excellence. I had to strike a balance between discipline and empathy, strategy and flexibility, and innovation and tradition.

Special Agent Duties

The agents I supervised were highly trained and skilled and were dedicated to law enforcement. These agents were responsible for investigating and handling a wide range of criminal activities within the agency's jurisdiction.

My agents underwent thorough, ongoing training and extensive background checks before joining the unit. They each had developed unique investigative and enforcement skills that allowed them to carry out complex undercover operations to fight crimes such as terrorism, drug trafficking, cybercrime, financial fraud, and organized crime.

The agents also frequently collaborate with other law enforcement agencies on cases of national or international significance, making their roles crucial for safeguarding national security and enforcing federal laws. They often faced significant risks, but they also had a strong dedication and commitment to their work.

Special Agents were exempt from the Fair Labor Standards Act and instead received Law Enforcement Availability Pay (LEAP). This increases the base salary by 25%, based on approximately ten hours of work each day. Any hours beyond ten are voluntary, effectively representing extra time and effort contributed to the government.

Agents didn't punch a time clock, and working over 50 hours a week was normal. When you were assigned to conduct an investigation, hours didn't matter. You worked whatever hours it took, including weekends, holidays, and overnight shifts. You ate and slept when you had the time. It was common to work on an investigation, which would take you away from home for days or weeks at a time.

All agents carried a "go bag" with them in the trunk of their assigned government vehicle. It typically contained essential items for various situations, such as active shooter incidents or emergencies. Some everyday items included were ammunition, spare magazines, and a first aid kit containing basic medical supplies such as bandages, gauze pads, and pain relievers. You had a flashlight, handcuffs, restraints, and clothes such as pants, shirts, underwear, and socks.

These items ensured that we were prepared for any situation we may encounter while on duty.

For any trips that may take longer out of town, you searched for a Walmart. At least you could get a few extra things to get you through until you got back home.

Linda understood when I had to go out of town for days or weeks at a time. However, some younger agents who had recently married were experiencing problems. That was just a few occasions because the majority of my agents were fine.

Requirements of an SA

A Special Agent must have excellent writing skills, along with the ability to think quickly and draw logical conclusions.

The mindset of an agent encompasses several key principles, including critical thinking. Agents had to make rapid decisions based on limited information, often under high-stress conditions.

Agents must possess problem-solving skills, as they analyze evidence and develop hypotheses to solve crimes, which requires a strong analytical mindset.

They were expected to cultivate an investigative mindset, which encompassed documenting evidence, assessing information, and comprehending the origin of the material.

It may not be immediately apparent, but agents require psychological insight, where they frequently employ psychological principles to comprehend the minds of both perpetrators and victims, which is essential for resolving complex cases. These skills and principles are crucial for conducting effective investigations and ensuring justice.

Stress

Let's acknowledge that working long shifts and extended hours can sometimes be challenging, especially when trying to balance time between work and family. It's common for agents to feel stressed and struggle to take time off for loved ones, which can lead to conflicts. Remember, stress is a natural part of life, and agents need to find ways to manage and lessen its effects, ensuring a healthier and happier balance for themselves and their families.

The stress of being a special agent was multifaceted, encompassing unpredictable hours and irregular shifts. The work environment was high-stress, requiring us to remain vigilant and prepared for potential threats at all times. Our job required rigorous training, strict physical fitness standards, and the potential for exposure to hazardous situations.

We often responded to risky and usually unfamiliar situations, frequently encountering unstable or unpredictable individuals, some of whom may pose a threat to our safety.

We also underwent psychological stress stemming from responsibilities like supporting victims or conducting investigations at crime scenes.

Nowadays, agents face intense scrutiny from the public. This can lead to stress while performing the duties.

While on duty, agents must always be prepared to defend themselves and respond quickly to a situation.

In federal law enforcement, male and female agents encounter different challenges and societal perceptions.

Even with initiatives to diversify the workforce, women remain a small minority of federal law enforcement officers, and few carry firearms.

I've observed that some male agents often perceive female agents as lacking certain masculine qualities, such as objectivity and assertiveness.

Public perceptions still often cling to traditional gender stereotypes, impacting female roles in law enforcement. I recall occasions when a female agent accompanied me; despite her asking the questions, people always looked at and addressed me.

After retiring from the federal government, I was aware of ongoing efforts to improve gender diversity in federal law enforcement. What has been done, I don't know.

My current issue is that I haven't conducted enough research on this topic to provide a clear explanation.

Being an agent was one of the most prestigious and dangerous occupations in the world. It takes specialized skills and a deep commitment to the job to be successful in the field.

There were times when agents had the chance to step in and lend a helping hand during disaster and recovery efforts after a crisis. We worked closely with local agencies to coordinate relief and recovery activities, ensuring everything flowed more smoothly and effectively. We also happily participated in humanitarian relief missions, providing medical personnel and supplies to support communities affected by natural disasters or civil unrest.

Agents have to possess a certain level of psychological preparedness to carry out their duties effectively. Being able to cope with the psychological strain that comes with the job is key to success. Agents must maintain their mental composure to make decisions quickly and accurately in high-pressure situations. They must also have the mental strength and resilience to deal with potentially traumatic events and the stress of long-term assignments.

Again, being an agent can profoundly affect a person's family and personal life. They often spend long stretches away from home, which can strain relationships. The stress and risks of the job may cause feelings of loneliness and disconnection. Furthermore, the job's demands can make it challenging to maintain a healthy work-life balance, leaving little time for family and leisure.

Chapter 2

Criminal Alien Program (CAP)

My first assignment in New Orleans was to supervise the CAP. This unit was entrusted with overseeing the states of Louisiana, Arkansas, Mississippi, Tennessee, and Alabama, which comprised our designated area of responsibility (AOR).

CAP included six agents and me, and one of our roles was to start removal (deportation) procedures against criminal aliens who were here illegally. We collaborated closely with state and local law enforcement agencies and inspected all jails and prisons within our Area of Responsibility (AOR).

We identified non-citizens held in detention and initiated deportation procedures to remove them from the United States. This involved conducting thorough interviews to evaluate their deportability. We also carried out investigations and prosecuted individuals for immigration violations in partnership with the U.S. Attorney's Office.

We also apprehended and detained individuals unlawfully present in the United States. We had to identify, investigate, and apprehend at-large "criminal aliens" convicted of drug trafficking, violent crimes, sex offenses, human trafficking, and smuggling.

During our investigations, we issued subpoenas to banks, phone companies, and internet service providers, and subsequently gathered extensive data to assess whether a criminal violation had occurred.

We traveled frequently, mainly within our AOR, but our investigations sometimes included trips across the U.S., Mexico, and Canada to conduct interviews and interrogations of known criminal aliens.

My unit also helped the ICE Enforcement and Removal Operations (ERO) in their mission to keep our homeland safe. We worked together to identify, arrest, and remove individuals who pose a threat to the integrity of U.S. immigration laws. This included focusing on apprehending incarcerated aliens across federal, state, and local levels, as well as at-large criminal aliens.

We issued ICE detainers on illegal aliens whom the agency had probable cause to believe are removable from the U.S. and were currently in federal, state, or local law enforcement agency custody. An immigration detainer is a request from ICE that asks a federal, state, or local law enforcement agency, including jails, prisons, or other confinement facilities, to notify ICE as soon as possible before releasing the individual. It requested to hold the alien for up to 48 hours beyond the time they would ordinarily be released, so that we had time to assume custody under federal immigration law.

We only lodge immigration detainers after establishing probable cause to believe that the alien is removable, typically following a court conviction for one or more crimes, and usually when the alien poses a threat to public safety or national security. The crimes were for being convicted of burglaries, robberies, kidnapping, homicide, sexual assault, weapons offenses, drug trafficking, and human trafficking.

Managing the CAP unit was demanding, but all agents were experienced and professional, requiring very little oversight.

Working in the CAP unit was sometimes exciting. We pursued criminal aliens evading law enforcement and carried out interviews with them. It was the perfect environment to hone interview techniques and collect evidence for criminal cases.

Arresting individuals was part of our duties, including executing arrest and search warrants. Each day, there's a risk of encountering someone trying to harm you, often leading to confrontations with those you're arresting.

Keep in mind, if we had a subject we were pursuing who was a high-risk, like someone with a significant criminal background, known for violence, and using firearms, we would prepare a team of agents before entering a residence or business to make the arrest. Even then, there would be other agents available, and every possible contingency would be planned for before entry.

Conducting Surveillance

Carrying out surveillance required balancing the need for information with the safeguarding of individuals' civil liberties. We made sure that all surveillance activities were justified and aligned with established principles and operational protocols. This involved clearly defining the scope of surveillance, ensuring there was reasonable suspicion, and following legal frameworks to prevent unreasonable searches and seizures.

On certain occasions, surveillance was carried out overtly through visible means, such as CCTV cameras, or covertly via techniques including wiretapping and undercover operations. Additionally, we utilized modern technologies, including drones and sophisticated camera systems, which enhanced our ability to collect evidence.

Recognize that ethical considerations were central to our surveillance. We ensured that our practices did not violate constitutionally protected rights.

Conducting surveillance played a crucial role in helping us combat crime, conduct thorough investigations, and maintain public safety. Whether it's tracking suspects, gathering evidence, or monitoring suspicious activities, surveillance techniques were among the most reliable tools.

My unit also investigated federal violations related to

immigration, human trafficking, narcotics, terrorism, general crime, and counterintelligence, and the agents could be deployed anywhere in the world if needed.

The CAP agents received training in various skills, including firearms, defensive tactics, physical restraint techniques, crime scene processing, suspect interviewing, protective service details, and specialized driving techniques. Maintaining good physical shape and functional fitness was essential.

On numerous occasions, we conducted undercover operations, executed arrest warrants, search warrants, and conducted surveillance, as well as wiretaps. We were occasionally deployed on marine vessels, worked with special forces, and were assigned to assist the U.S. Secret Service on presidential details.

Conducting Search Warrants

The entry of a search warrant was exciting, but there was more to it than kicking in doors and searching residences or businesses. Most search warrant executions involved numerous administrative tasks that must be performed. These include photographing the scene before and after the search, sometimes sketching it, photographing where evidence was recovered, recording the time and place of evidence collection, tracking who was present and what they did, and providing a list of all seized items to the property owner.

Afterward, the real work began when you returned to your office, logged all items into the evidence room, and spent the rest of the day/night drafting all necessary reports of investigations. Otherwise, prepare your case for court.

We often worked in hazardous conditions, and there was no such thing as a typical workday. Each day was different, and you could find yourself testifying in federal court, executing a search warrant, or conducting surveillance.

Handling Informants

At times, you would meet with your confidential informant to collect information on illegal activities or intelligence, or you could be involved in making an arrest. Then, you met with your colleagues back at the office to catch up on paperwork and discuss the day's events.

Let me talk briefly about the process of meeting with an informant. Before an agent meets with an informant, several steps are involved to ensure the integrity and reliability of the information provided.

To meet with an informant, an agent must first conduct vetting to ensure the informant is reliable and possesses the necessary knowledge. This includes verifying the informant's background, their motivations for providing information, and any relevant criminal histories.

We must then formally authorize the informant to engage in activities that could involve illegal behavior, such as buying illicit drugs from the target of a drug-trafficking investigation. We would document the reasons and risks associated with the informant's involvement in these activities for the record.

The informant was later asked to give a written acknowledgment of the agency's instructions regarding risks, regulations, and responsibilities. This was crucial to maintain the informant's trustworthiness and reliability.

Informants were assigned a case agent, who carefully monitored their activities during cooperation to ensure they stayed within the approved scope and avoided any unauthorized activities.

The case agent kept records of the informant's activities and any authorized actions taken. This documentation was crucial for maintaining the integrity of the investigation and ensuring the protection of the informant.

The meeting with an informant was a process that required careful planning and adherence to legal and ethical guidelines to ensure the effectiveness of the investigation.

Building relationships with sources and informants was

crucial for success in conducting intelligence work. An agent needs to develop and sustain these relationships to gather valuable information. This demands tact, discretion, and knowledge of various cultures and customs. Agents must communicate effectively with individuals from diverse backgrounds and situations, often in challenging environments.

In August 2003, I attended a weeklong DHS undercover school in Potomac, MD. The course instructed on effective recruitment and utilization of informants, identifying safety considerations, and unique problems associated with undercover work. It addressed the psychological challenges of undercover work, identifying difficult undercover situations and demonstrating methods to resolve them. We discussed prosecutorial guidelines, regulations, and entrapment issues in the context of risk management for undercover operations.

We also discussed key issues related to supervising undercover units and staff. The course was very informative, covering a lot of material in just one week.

Training was essential in the CAP due to updates in policies and procedures affecting the government, local jails, and state prisons. We needed to stay current with the latest interview and interrogation techniques, along with all recent changes in immigration laws. For my unit's agents and me, training was an ongoing requirement.

CHAPTER 3

Investigating Child Exploitation

First, I want to acknowledge that this is one of the most challenging units to serve in. Cases involving child exploitation are among the most urgent and emotionally taxing within law enforcement and child protection. Agents investigating these cases face not only technical difficulties in collecting evidence and prosecuting offenders but also significant moral and psychological burdens. Their reflections demonstrate a strong commitment to justice, but also highlight the considerable toll that such work takes on their personal and professional lives.

When you're sifting through evidence, you're not just looking at data; you're seeing moments of a child's life, sometimes the worst moments they'll ever experience. The gravity of that is never lost. Knowing that our intervention can mean the difference between continued harm and safety for a child makes the stakes very real, very immediate.

The investigation of child exploitation cases, including offenses involving illegal content, is a critically important field tasked with protecting vulnerable individuals and upholding justice. These investigations must be conducted with utmost sensitivity, professionalism, and adherence to legal procedures. I will outline the typical protocols, ethical considerations, and challenges inherent in investigating such cases, with an emphasis on child safety and the responsibilities of law enforcement and society.

Before starting any investigation, it is crucial to understand the legal definitions and frameworks related to child exploitation offenses. While laws vary between countries, most criminalize the creation, distribution, possession, and viewing of illegal content involving minors. Additionally, international treaties like the United Nations Convention on the Rights of the Child influence national policies and law enforcement efforts. The investigation of cases involving child exploitation requires meticulous adherence to protocols designed to protect victims, preserve evidence, and respect legal rights.

Initial Steps

Cases may begin with reports from victims, guardians, teachers, social workers, or tips from the public. Anonymous reporting channels and hotlines are common. The immediate priority is to secure potential evidence, including digital devices, online communications, and physical materials, without compromising or losing it. Ensuring the safety of the affected child is paramount. Removing them from harm, providing medical and psychological support, and initiating child welfare involvement are early actions.

Considering the widespread occurrence of cybercrimes, digital forensics plays a pivotal role in investigative processes. Specialized units are tasked with identifying and analyzing devices, accounts, and networks involved in criminal activities, tracing digital footprints through metadata, file logs, and communications. Employing encryption-breaking tools and data recovery software enables access to concealed or deleted files. International collaboration is crucial for tracking the cross-border sharing and dissemination of information.

Interviewing Victims and Witnesses

Interviews must be conducted by specially trained professionals, often in child-friendly environments. Techniques are designed to minimize trauma and avoid leading questions or coercion. Support services, including psychologists and victim advocates, are integrated throughout the process.

Investigators analyze evidence to identify suspects, often involving complex digital tracing and coordination with multiple agencies. Search warrants and legal authorizations are required for access to private information. Apprehension is done with consideration for community safety and the rights of suspects.

No single agency can address child exploitation cases alone.

Effective investigations depend on collaboration across sectors. Law enforcement collaborates with child protective services, healthcare professionals, educators, and non-governmental organizations. International and inter-jurisdictional cooperation is crucial, given the prevalence of internet-based offenses. Public awareness campaigns help encourage reporting and educate communities about the risks and signs of exploitation.

Investigating these cases presents profound ethical responsibilities. Protecting the dignity and privacy of victims is essential; investigators must avoid unnecessary exposure or re-traumatization. Handling sensitive evidence requires secure and confidential procedures. Due process must be observed to protect the rights of all parties involved. Investigators face significant obstacles, including technological sophistication, jurisdictional hurdles, and the psychological toll of working on such cases.

Exposure to disturbing material can affect investigators' mental health, requiring access to counseling and support. Agencies must foster a culture of care and resilience among staff.

The investigators working for Immigration and Customs Enforcement who work child pornography and exploitation cases nationwide must reckon with the short- and long-term psychological impact of repeatedly being exposed to images of helpless children being violated. The emotional strain of working child exploitation cases cannot be overstated. Exposure to graphic material, heart-wrenching victim statements, and the realities of abuse leaves lasting impressions.

Agents in this division sometimes undergo a psychological evaluation to ensure they are still mentally capable of working cases involving child pornography.

The caseload is overwhelming. Each case requires that investigators view acts of brutality inflicted on the most vulnerable in our society.

Agents assigned say they find ways to cope, from deciding when and how to look at the images to finding outlets to relieve the resulting stress. Some commiserate with their fellow agents. The agents try to limit the amount of time they look at a file, but they're required to give it enough attention to determine whether the images or videos depict child exploitation.

I myself had a rule I used when I was assigned to the task force. I didn't start or end the day by looking at the images, so I had time to unwind before heading home.

Every agent handles the delicate task in their own way. Before sitting in front of his computer, Allen turns on a television that serves as background noise. The show itself doesn't really matter.

Proactive measures are vital to protect children and prevent exploitation. Education for children, parents, and educators about online safety, privacy, and the risks of digital communication. Regular monitoring and reporting mechanisms within schools and community organizations. Technological safeguards include parental controls and safe browsing tools. Encouraging open dialogue and trust with children so they feel safe and secure in reporting their concerns.

Investigating instances of child exploitation requires meticulous professionalism, compassion, and legal expertise. By adhering to established protocols, engaging in interdisciplinary collaboration, and promoting community awareness, society can strive to ensure the protection of children and guarantee justice for the victims. The obligation to safeguard the vulnerable rests collectively with law enforcement, professionals, and the public.

To sum it up, working on child exploitation cases is a calling that demands courage, empathy, and unwavering dedication. Agents who undertake this work are driven by a commitment to justice and the well-being of the most vulnerable members of society. Their reflections reveal lives marked by challenge and sacrifice, but also by moments of profound impact and hope.

As technology and society continue to evolve, the fight against child exploitation constantly adapts. Yet, the dedication of those who protect and serve remains strong, showcasing the incredible resilience of the human spirit even in the most difficult times.

CHAPTER 4

Arkansas Lawyer Case

When I started my supervisory duties in the New Orleans investigations office, many employees in New Orleans and the five-state area I served were unfamiliar with me. No one knew who I was.

With that in mind, in July 2002, the Deputy District Director for Investigations asked me to conduct an undercover investigation with the U.S. Immigration Office of Professional Responsibility (OPR) from our Headquarters office. OPR is the internal affairs division of the federal government, and OPR agents investigate allegations of misconduct made against government employees.

As a new employee, I was asked to work undercover and assist OPR with their investigation in Arkansas. OPR had received information alleging that an Immigration Supervisory Special Agent was involved in fraud and misconduct at one of the Arkansas immigration offices. My task was to investigate whether the immigration supervisor was engaged in any misconduct. As I stated before, I had never met the supervisor or special agents working in and around the target area.

Following my visit to Arkansas, I convened with investigators from OPR and the Federal Bureau of Investigation (FBI) to receive an update on the case. The briefing lasted several hours, during which I endeavored to understand the purported role of the supervisor and other individuals implicated.

It was reported that an attorney specializing in immigration law was practicing in Springdale, AR, and he was promising foreign nationals who were in the U.S. illegally that he could file the necessary paperwork and petitions for them to obtain immigration benefits. The attorney would lie and tell the undocumented individuals that submitting this paperwork would allow them to live and work in the U.S. legally. All they had to do was pay the necessary fee to cover the cost of preparing the documents.

This attorney was aware that those in the U.S. illegally had no relief from deportation other than to self-deport. The attorney was Hispanic himself, and that was why I could not believe he would treat other Hispanics that way, stealing money from them.

This attorney was intentionally committing fraud by scamming undocumented immigrants into thinking he could secure them a legal benefit. The attorney charged each illegal $2000 to prepare and file the paperwork. He prepared approximately 10 to 12 documents a day at the immigration office in Dallas, Texas.

Luckily, we developed a female informant who cooperated

with us. She worked directly for the suspect attorney. She told us that she believed an immigration supervisory special agent from an immigration office would visit regularly and have lunch with the attorney. The informant was one of two women working in the attorney's office. She suspected that the immigration supervisor was referring potential clients to the attorney. However, she had no evidence to support this. She did know that illegal Hispanic families were constantly pouring into the attorney's office seeking relief.

The informant mentioned to us that she and the other women working in the attorney's office didn't get along well. She explained that the other female employee would schedule appointments for undocumented individuals to meet with the attorney and then assist them in filling out an application for a permanent resident card. If approved, this would allow the individual to live and work in the United States as a permanent resident. This female employee, who had worked in the office for years, must have known that the attorney's actions were incorrect.

After preparing the paperwork for the undocumented individuals, the employee would then prepare it for the attorney's signature and filing. Again, the issue was that the undocumented individuals did not qualify for permanent resident status, a green card, or any government benefits. They were paying this attorney for false beliefs or hopes. They didn't know any better. They only knew what an attorney had advised them.

After filling out the application, the attorney would charge undocumented individuals $2,000 in cash, to be paid up front. The informant stated that the female employee would collect the money from them and later mail the applications to the U.S. Immigration processing center, located in Dallas, Texas. The informant provided us with all the names and addresses of individuals who had already paid money for the scam and were awaiting a hearing from the attorney.

One of the documents the attorney used was a Form I-485, also known as the Adjustment of Status Application. It is used to apply for lawful permanent resident status in the United States. You can submit Form I-485 if you are eligible for a green card and entered the United States on a valid non-immigrant visa. The form collects basic information about the applicant's identity and checks for grounds of inadmissibility. The standard fee for filling out this form was approximately $235. The problem was that none of the people qualified for the benefit and status. They were paying for nothing because they were going to be denied.

The attorney knew that these undocumented individuals would not qualify for this status, and all their applications would eventually be denied. He deliberately lied to these illegals and filed the applications, knowing they would be rejected. However, he collected their $ 2,000, filed the application with the $235 filing fee, and then waited six to twelve weeks for it to be denied.

After receiving the denial notice, he would notify the illegals and offer an apology. The attorney deliberately gave false hope to these individuals, knowing that no immigration relief was available to them. He was the kind of individual who didn't care about people's feelings because he was getting his money for nothing.

I worked on this investigation for several months. However, my primary assignment was to find out if the immigration supervisor had helped the attorney commit fraud against undocumented immigrants. If he was involved, I needed to understand how much he knew and if he received any money for his role.

I had our informant review the office files to determine if any payments were made to the immigration supervisor in any way. The informant was unable to find any documentation.

After completing the investigation, it was determined that no evidence showed the immigration supervisor was involved with the attorney in this scam. I had proof that the supervisor was good friends with the attorney and had attended several outdoor cookouts at the attorney's residence. Other than that, there was nothing.

I contacted the supervisor and informed him of the allegation.

I ended up interviewing him on two separate occasions and told him that charges were being filed against his attorney friend. He became visibly upset about his friend's involvement, stating he couldn't believe it. No charges were filed against the immigration supervisor, and management was notified of my findings.

As for the attorney, we ultimately executed a search warrant at his office, collecting the necessary paperwork to substantiate our case. We matched the documents with the actual documents he sent to the Dallas Examinations branch.

The attorney practiced immigration law in Springdale and Van Buren, AR. After gathering sufficient evidence to substantiate our fraud case, we charged him in the U.S. District Court in Ft Smith, AR., for a scheme to obtain unauthorized employment authorization cards for ineligible aliens.

During court proceedings, the attorney appeared before a U.S. Magistrate charged with conspiring to bribe a public official and conspiring to commit document fraud. The attorney pleaded not guilty and was released on a $5,000 bond pending further proceedings.

We continued our investigation, collecting more evidence against the attorney. During this time, the attorney returned to court and pleaded guilty to both charges. He was sentenced to one year in prison and gave up his Arkansas law license, which meant he could no longer practice law in Arkansas.

The investigation continued, following the lead of an immigration attorney practicing in Dallas, TX. To make a long story short, he was charged and pleaded guilty to the exact charges as our Arkansas attorney. He received the same sentence and is no longer allowed to practice law.

I worked on several spin-off cases from this criminal case. It appeared to be a small network of attorneys who were taking advantage of illegal immigrants who were attempting to find a way to stay in the U.S. legally. These particular attorneys were exploiting the fears and hopes of undocumented immigrants.

CHAPTER 5

Name Changed March 1, 2003

The Federal Government Historical Archives provided the information below. This change occurred while I was assigned to the New Orleans Criminal Investigations unit.

On March 1, 2003, a significant realignment occurred within federal agencies. Before that date, the U.S. Immigration and Naturalization Service (INS) was part of the U.S. Department of Justice (DOJ) from 1940 to 2003.

Known as INS, the agency ceased to exist under that name on March 1, 2003, when most of its functions were transferred to three new entities: U.S. Citizenship and Immigration Services (USCIS), U.S. Immigration and Customs Enforcement (ICE), and U.S. Customs and Border Protection (CBP), all within the newly formed U.S. Department of Homeland Security (DHS), as part of a major government reorganization after the September 11, 2001, attacks.

The change was merely a title change, and all the laws remained unchanged. U.S. Customs criminal investigators joined U.S. Immigration criminal Investigators, and we shared the load of the legacy INS laws and the U.S. Customs laws.

As of March 1, 2003, we changed from the U.S. Immigration and Naturalization Service to the U.S. Immigration and Customs Enforcement (ICE).

In March 2003, I became a founding member of the Department of Homeland Security (DHS), Immigration and Customs Enforcement (ICE). I continued my assignment in the New Orleans office as a Supervisory Special Agent.

Homeland Security Investigations (HSI) is the principal investigative arm of the U.S. Department of Homeland Security, responsible for investigating transnational crime and threats, specifically those criminal organizations that exploit the global infrastructure through which international trade, travel, and finance move.

HSI's workforce of over 10,400 employees comprises more than 7,100 Special Agents assigned to 220 cities throughout the United States, as well as 80 overseas locations in 53 countries. HSI's international presence represents DHS's most prominent investigative law enforcement presence abroad and one of the largest global footprints in U.S. law enforcement.

HSI criminal investigators, also referred to as special agents, conduct criminal and civil investigations involving national security threats, terrorism, drug smuggling, child exploitation, human trafficking, illegal arms export, financial crimes, identity fraud, benefit fraud, commercial fraud, and more.

ICE is a global leader in investigating international crimes, including transnational crime and violations of U.S. Customs and Immigration laws. Our investigations are diverse and wide-ranging, focusing on illegal movements of people, goods, money, contraband, weapons, and sensitive technology. ICE plays a crucial role in combating cybercrime, including dark net and other cyber-related criminal investigations.

ICE's worldwide reach and operational flexibility allow it to safeguard the country's digital borders and track down international cybercriminals.

Our cases often start by looking into individuals who violate U.S. laws. But we don't stop there, ICE builds complex cases against the most sophisticated criminal networks that operate globally and pose the greatest threat to our security.

As previously mentioned, ICE special agents conduct criminal and civil investigations involving national security threats, terrorism, drug smuggling, child exploitation, human trafficking, illegal arms export, financial crimes, identity fraud, benefit fraud, commercial fraud, and much more.

We also worked very closely with federal, state, and local law enforcement agencies, including the FBI, DEA, and U.S. Marshals Service, as well as state police and county sheriff's departments. In addition, special agents have the opportunity to participate in special task forces or fugitive operations teams.

CHAPTER 6

Unlawful Entry

What occurs when Immigration Agents arrest an undocumented individual who entered the United States unlawfully? This brief overview outlines the process and possible objections.

Initial Apprehension

Under the Immigration and Nationality Act (INA), when someone is caught crossing the border or found in the U.S. without proper authorization, agents have the authority to detain them on suspicion of violating immigration laws. They will conduct a preliminary interview to verify the individual's identity, nationality, and method of entry.

The process varies based on factors such as location and the individual's background. Individuals with prior immigration violations or criminal records may face different procedures than those with no previous convictions.

Agents will utilize databases, such as the Automated Biometric Identification System (IDENT), to verify identities and check for existing warrants, thereby informing decisions about detention and subsequent actions.

Detention and Processing

After apprehension, individuals are usually taken to an ICE detention facility for processing. During this stage, biometric data collection confirms their identity and checks for prior immigration or criminal records, which play a key role in determining eligibility for relief or release.

Detention conditions and duration depend on individual circumstances and facility capacity. Facilities must adhere to Department of Homeland Security (DHS) standards regarding living conditions, medical care, and communication with legal representatives. However, reports of inadequate conditions have raised concerns and prompted calls for reform. Extended detention without timely hearings has also led to legal challenges, raising constitutional questions about due process.

Expedited Removal

Expedited removal enables immigration authorities to swiftly deport individuals who are caught crossing the border without authorization. It primarily applies to individuals detained within 100 miles of the border who cannot demonstrate that they have been in the U.S. continuously for at least 14 days. This process skips immigration court proceedings unless individuals express fear of persecution or torture, which then triggers a credible fear interview conducted by an asylum officer.

This procedure aims to enhance border security by facilitating swift deportations and deterring illegal entry. Agents evaluate whether individuals qualify for expedited removal and are required to inform them of their rights, including the option to request protection if they fear returning to their country of origin. If a fear of return is expressed, a credible fear assessment will be conducted to determine if the individual qualifies for asylum or other forms of protection.

Possible Criminal Charges

Individuals apprehended crossing the border without authorization may face criminal charges under U.S. federal law. Illegal entry makes it a crime to enter or attempt to enter the U.S. at unauthorized times or places.

First-time offenders may be subject to fines and up to six months of imprisonment. Repeat offenders can face felony charges for illegal re-entry, with penalties ranging from two years in prison to longer sentences for individuals with prior convictions for aggravated felonies.

The decision to pursue criminal charges is made by U.S.

Attorneys, who take into account the circumstances of each case and the individual's history. Factors such as previous deportations, criminal records, or involvement in smuggling impact prosecutorial discretion.

Enforcement priorities differ among administrations, with some focusing on criminal prosecution for border crossings, while others prioritize civil immigration processes.

Immigration Court Hearings

Detained individuals may undergo immigration court hearings, conducted by judges from the Executive Office for Immigration Review, to decide whether they can stay in the U.S. or must be removed. These proceedings involve DHS attorneys advocating for the deportation of individuals.

During hearings, individuals can present evidence and testimony to support claims for relief, such as asylum, cancellation of removal, or adjustment of status. The burden of proof rests with the individual, making legal representation crucial.

Judges consider factors like family ties, duration of residence, and humanitarian circumstances when making decisions. Outcomes vary, with some individuals granted relief and others ordered to be removed.

Future Entry Restrictions

Individuals who are removed or voluntarily depart after unlawfully crossing the border often face future entry restrictions. These restrictions, arising from the INA, significantly affect the ability to return to the U.S. legally.

The most common consequence is a re-entry bar, which ranges from five to 20 years, depending on the circumstances of removal and any previous immigration violations.

Re-entry bars are strictly enforced to deter unauthorized re-entry. Individuals may apply for a waiver, which requires proof of extreme hardship affecting a U.S. citizen or lawful permanent resident family member.

The waiver process is complex and usually requires legal assistance. Violating re-entry restrictions can result in severe penalties, including criminal prosecution and permanent inadmissibility.

Voluntary Departure

In some cases, individuals caught crossing the border may be eligible for voluntary departure, which allows them to leave the U.S. at their own expense without a formal removal order. This option avoids the re-entry bars that accompany deportation orders.

Voluntary departure may occur before or after immigration court proceedings. Before proceedings, individuals typically have up to 120 days to exit, whereas those allowed to depart afterward usually face a shorter period, often around 60 days. To be eligible, individuals must demonstrate good moral character, possess the financial resources necessary for departure, and comply with the order to leave. Specific criminal convictions, such as aggravated felonies, result in disqualification.

Although voluntary departure avoids more severe repercussions, failing to depart within the given time frame can result in fines, a 10-year ban on re-entry, and the conversion of the voluntary departure order into a removal order.

Seeking legal counsel is often crucial for successfully navigating this process and ensuring compliance with immigration laws.

ICE agents are out on the streets every day, working hard to keep our communities safe by finding, arresting, and removing criminal aliens and immigration violators from our neighborhoods.

ICE does not need judicial warrants to make arrests. Like all other law enforcement officers, ICE agents can initiate consensual encounters and speak with people, briefly detain aliens when they have reasonable suspicion that the aliens are illegally present in the United States, and arrest people they believe are illegal aliens. ICE agents can also detain and search people crossing the border.

All illegals who violate U.S. immigration law are subject to arrest and detention, regardless of their criminal histories. Those with final orders of removal are removed from the United States.

ICE agents typically cannot show the warrants they are executing to people who aren't named or directly involved. This is often due to law enforcement sensitivities and privacy concerns that require officials to keep such information confidential.

Remember, ICE agents play a vital role that goes beyond just looking for criminal aliens. They are dedicated to identifying and apprehending removable aliens. Still, their responsibilities also extend to investigating transnational crime and focusing on individuals who might pose a risk to national security, public safety, or border security. This means ICE agents use a variety of enforcement strategies, including detaining those with criminal backgrounds and individuals seen as threats to public safety. Their work is crucial in keeping our communities safe and secure.

CHAPTER 7

Undocumented Migrants Working

Within the CAP unit, our investigation focused on cases concerning undocumented migrants employed within the United States. This topic is intricate and encompasses various dimensions, including legal, economic, and social considerations. Individuals from diverse backgrounds, encompassing all genders, arrive in the country seeking employment for a multitude of reasons, such as financial necessity, family reunification, or fleeing persecution in search of improved living conditions.

Migrants who work in the U.S. without proper authorization are commonly referred to as "undocumented workers." U.S. labor laws require employees to have a valid immigration status and documentation, such as a work visa, permanent residency, or citizenship. Those who work without this authorization may face risks, including deportation, limited legal protections, and barriers to healthcare and social services.

Undocumented workers may have less protection from workplace abuses such as wage theft, unsafe working conditions, or discrimination, since reporting these issues could risk exposing their status. These individuals often work in low-wage, physically demanding jobs, including in agriculture, hospitality, domestic work, and construction, which can make them more susceptible to exploitation.

The stigma attached to being undocumented can affect mental health and hinder integration into local communities. Undocumented workers may also have limited access to healthcare and may work without adequate safety measures.

While all undocumented workers face challenges, females may encounter unique barriers and risks. Female undocumented workers are at risk of facing harassment or abuse in the workplace, often with fewer avenues for reporting or seeking help. Many undocumented women work to support families both in the U.S. and abroad, balancing caregiving duties with employment challenges.

The debates in the U.S. about immigration reform, pathways to legal status, and protections for undocumented workers continue. Some states and localities have implemented policies that offer greater access to healthcare, education, and driver's licenses, regardless of a person's immigration status. Still, federal law remains the primary source of immigration policy, and comprehensive reform has yet to be achieved.

It is argued by many that undocumented individuals contribute significantly to the U.S. economy and society, despite facing numerous challenges.

Using Fraudulent Documents

The problem of undocumented migrants using fraudulent documents to find jobs is a complex issue involving social, legal, and economic aspects. Across the nation, some migrants attempt to secure employment by submitting counterfeit or altered documents, such as forged Social Security cards, work permits, or other identification, to employers. Several factors motivate this behavior, which has significant implications for the individuals involved and the broader community.

Some undocumented migrants in the U.S. may use counterfeit or stolen Social Security cards to provide a valid number on employment forms. Some migrants may present forged work authorization documents, such as fake immigration visas or counterfeit green cards, which are often used to prove employment eligibility falsely.

During the hiring process, individuals may present altered or counterfeit government-issued IDs, such as driver's licenses or ID cards. In contrast, others may use counterfeit birth certificates to claim citizenship or establish a legal presence in the country.

The reasons for using fraudulent documents can differ, but many illegal immigrants are driven by difficult economic situations, limited legal job options, or a pressing need to support their families. Additionally, strict immigration policies or slow processing times for legal documents often motivate individuals to seek alternative ways to find employment.

However, using fake documents to get a job can create serious problems for both the worker and the employer. If someone is caught using false papers, they might face deportation, criminal charges, or fines. Similarly, employers who knowingly hire undocumented workers could encounter legal issues, such as hefty penalties and sanctions. It's always best to stick to honest and legal methods when seeking employment or hiring. The discovery of fraudulent documentation can result in immediate termination of employment and make it challenging to secure future employment opportunities.

Identity Theft

There are many cases where individuals will obtain documents using stolen identities, which can cause harm to the actual owners of the credentials.

Employers are legally obligated to verify the identity and employment eligibility of job candidates. Systems such as E-Verify in the United States are designed to check the authenticity of documentation provided by prospective employees. Employers must remain vigilant to avoid inadvertently hiring individuals who present fraudulent documents.

Efforts to prevent the use of fraudulent documents include implementing stricter document verification procedures, providing training for employers, and conducting education and outreach programs to inform both employers and job seekers about the legal risks and alternatives.

The use of fraudulent documents by undocumented immigrants to find work is a complex issue. It highlights personal struggles and larger systemic problems, while also raising legal and ethical questions for our society. Addressing this situation requires fair policies, robust verification systems, and open conversations to ensure fairness, safety, and equal opportunities for all individuals in the workforce.

Hiring Undocumented Workers

The hiring of undocumented workers by businesses is a subject of complex legal, economic, and social debate. In the United States, the presence and employment of undocumented migrants have significant implications for labor markets, policy, and society at large.

Many businesses, particularly in sectors like agriculture, hospitality, construction, manufacturing, and domestic services, are drawn to hiring undocumented workers for several reasons. Specific industries are struggling to find enough workers with the necessary legal skills to perform physically demanding or low-wage jobs. Undocumented workers may accept lower wages and fewer benefits, reducing costs for employers. Then, the flexibility and availability of a labor force that can be hired seasonally or on short notice appeals to sectors with variable demand.

Some businesses are willing to risk penalties due to limited enforcement capacity or lax regulatory oversight.

The decision to employ undocumented workers carries both potential advantages and significant risks. There are some legal risks and penalties. Employers face serious consequences if they are found in violation of immigration or labor laws. Penalties can include fines ranging from hundreds to thousands of dollars per unauthorized employee, loss of business licenses or permits, and criminal charges in cases of repeated violations or egregious conduct.

Increased workplace raids, audits, and stiffer penalties are used to deter businesses from employing undocumented workers. The E-Verify program in the United States is one example of a tool designed to confirm work authorization more reliably.

E-Verify is a website operated by the United States Department of Homeland Security (DHS) that assists businesses in verifying the eligibility of their employees to work in the U.S., including both U.S. citizens and foreign nationals. It was first launched in 1996 as the Basic Pilot Program to stop employers from hiring individuals who had entered the country illegally and violated immigration laws.

In August 2007, the DHS began requiring all federal contractors and vendors to use E-Verify. The U.S. government operates this free, internet-based program. Although federal law does not mandate E-Verify for non-federal employees, some states have made it compulsory or adopted similar programs, while others have discouraged its use.

The issue of businesses hiring undocumented workers is multifaceted, extending beyond simple legal compliance to encompass ethical, economic, and human considerations. Solutions are rarely straightforward, requiring cooperation between government, business, and community stakeholders. As societies continue to grapple with the challenges and opportunities presented by undocumented labor, the hope remains for policies that strike a balance between economic needs, human rights, and the rule of law.

CHAPTER 8

Investigating Human Trafficking

Human trafficking constitutes a pervasive and deeply rooted global issue, affecting millions annually and undermining fundamental human rights such as dignity and liberty. In the United States, multiple agencies are charged with the responsibility of investigating and combating human trafficking, with U.S. Immigration and Customs Enforcement (ICE) playing a pivotal role. ICE agents operate within Homeland Security Investigations (HSI), an entity tasked explicitly with addressing crimes related to both labor and sexual exploitation. This discussion will elucidate how ICE agents conduct investigations into human trafficking, the challenges they face, the methods and tools they employ, and the broader initiatives aimed at combating trafficking.

Understanding Human Trafficking

Human trafficking is defined as the exploitation of individuals through force, fraud, or coercion for forced labor, sexual servitude, or both. Victims of trafficking may be men, women, or children, and traffickers prey on vulnerabilities such as poverty, lack of social support, and displacement. Trafficking networks often extend across borders and involve complex criminal organizations.

Common indicators of human trafficking include a person's lack of freedom of movement, deprivation of identification documents, threats of violence against the victim or their family, withholding wages or payments, manipulation through debt or false promises, and involvement in commercial sexual activities under duress.

ICE agents within HSI work diligently to detect, investigate, and dismantle trafficking operations. They strive to identify potential trafficking victims, follow up on leads and tips from the community, collect evidence, monitor activities, execute search warrants, and make necessary arrests, all with a strong commitment to protecting and serving the public.

Agents are trained to recognize the signs of trafficking and engage with victims sensitively and professionally. They often partner with victim support organizations to ensure that individuals rescued from trafficking situations receive medical, psychological, and legal assistance.

Agents employ a wide variety of investigative techniques to uncover human trafficking operations. Agents gather intelligence from diverse sources, including tip lines, informants, suspicious activity reports, and digital communications. They analyze patterns of movement, financial transactions, and social connections that may indicate trafficking.

Undercover assignments are also a critical tool in trafficking investigations. Agents may pose as buyers or traffickers to infiltrate criminal networks and obtain first-hand evidence of trafficking activities. Advanced surveillance methods, including wiretaps, electronic communications monitoring, and network analysis, are employed to track suspects and comprehend the structure of trafficking rings. ICE agents may utilize facial recognition software, data mining, and geolocation tools to follow leads and build cases.

ICE agents frequently participate in multi-agency task forces, such as the Anti-Trafficking Coordination Team Initiative (ACTeam), which combines resources from the Department of Justice, the FBI, and local law enforcement. These collaborations enhance the capacity to investigate and prosecute complex cases.

Investigating human trafficking presents unique challenges. Traffickers employ sophisticated methods to hide their operations, including frequent relocations, use of false documents, and operating through legitimate businesses. Victims may be reluctant to cooperate due to fear, trauma, or distrust of law enforcement. Building trust is essential. Trafficking cases are often transnational, requiring coordination across jurisdictions and languages. Cultural barriers and a lack of awareness can hamper the identification and rescue of victims. The emotional toll of working with traumatized individuals and confronting the realities of exploitation can be significant for agents.

ICE agents are not only responsible for investigating and prosecuting trafficking crimes but also for safeguarding the welfare of victims. Once individuals are rescued, agents work to ensure they are not treated as criminals, but as survivors in need of assistance.

Human trafficking is prosecuted under federal laws, mainly the Trafficking Victims Protection Act (TVPA) and related statutes. ICE agents support prosecutors by gathering evidence, interviewing witnesses, and preparing court cases for prosecution. Efforts to prosecute focus on holding traffickers responsible with strict penalties, ensuring victims receive restitution and justice, and preventing future trafficking through public awareness and proactive law enforcement. Convictions often rely on the testimony of victims and the evidence gathered during investigations. ICE agents play a vital role in supporting victims throughout the legal process.

International Collaboration

Human trafficking frequently crosses borders, requiring ICE agents to work with international partners. Through agreements, joint operations, and information sharing, agents help disrupt global trafficking networks and repatriate victims safely.

Collaborations may involve coordination with law enforcement agencies in source, transit, and destination countries, participation in INTERPOL initiatives, and training foreign law enforcement in best practices. These international efforts enhance ICE's capacity to address trafficking comprehensively.

ICE agents play a crucial role in the fight against human trafficking, balancing enforcement, victim protection, and prevention. Their work is challenging and often emotionally demanding, but essential for securing justice and safeguarding the vulnerable. Through investigation, collaboration, and community engagement, ICE agents strive to dismantle trafficking operations and restore freedom to those who have been exploited.

CHAPTER 9

The Story of a Human Smuggler

This is a true story that took place on the border of Mexico, involving a once-notorious smuggler. I have omitted names and other identifying details for the sake of privacy and respect for those involved. The information is based on interviews with all involved.

From a young age, this smuggler (known as a Coyote) watched the daily movement across the Rio Grande: workers, families, and children slipping into the night, driven by the hope of a better life. By his late twenties, he held various odd jobs on both sides, working as a mechanic, laborer, and driver, until his family's livelihood came to an abrupt end. That was when he first took payment to help two cousins cross the border. News spread fast, and his illegal business grew.

The Coyote's operations were never as glamorous as portrayed in movies. There were no cargo containers or hidden tunnels, only a web of borrowed vehicles, discreet phone calls, and trusted lookouts. He collaborated with a few local contacts, driven by loyalty or necessity. Each crossing involved careful planning, balancing border patrol schedules, river currents, and the constant danger of betrayal or detection.

In time, the coyote justified his choices. He saw himself not as a criminal, but as a facilitator, a bridge for those trapped on the wrong side of opportunity. He charged less than the cartels, took fewer risks with his passengers, and refused to carry weapons. He promised to keep people safe, and convinced himself that someone would do it, better him than the ruthless ones.

However, over time, the border started to change. Agents intensified their efforts to dismantle smuggling networks. Drones now flew overhead. Unmarked SUVs patrolled the highways. Agents, dressed in civilian clothes, blended into border towns, listening for leads.

A female Border Patrol Agent, raised in the same area as the coyote, understood both perspectives of the struggle —the hope for a new start and the pain of those left behind. After months of following faint leads, she had built a detailed file filled with anonymous tips, intercepted communications, and blurry images. The effort to capture the coyote was a collaborative operation involving local law enforcement.

On a morning in May, agents were tipped off by an informant that the coyote's van would be passing through a small, rural immigration checkpoint. The female agent stayed focused and led the team. Surveillance units shadowed the coyote's van from a discreet distance, noting the careful way he checked his mirrors, the indirect routes he favored, and the coded language he used during brief phone calls.

Late that afternoon, the coyote's van neared the checkpoint. He knew the risks and tried to remain invisible, avoiding eye contact and making no sudden movements, just another commuter on his way to work. Yet, ICE and Border Patrol agents were ready. At the signal, two vehicles flanked the coyote's van, lights flashing. The coyote pulled over, the weight of inevitability pressing on his shoulders.

The agents moved efficiently, separating the passengers and leading them to the waiting vehicles. The coyote recognized the female agent, her resolve evident in her posture. There was no violence, just the steady rhythm of procedure. Papers were checked, and questions were asked.

The coyote was placed in handcuffs. For the first time, he felt the full weight of his choices. The passengers, some weary, some grateful, others resentful, were transported to a processing center. Each would face their own uncertain future: some seeking asylum, others facing deportation, and a few perhaps disappearing into the complexities of the system.

Of course, the coyote's arrest made the local news. Some in the community called him a villain, while others referred to him as a necessary evil. His family faced the sting of public shame and the uncertainty of lost income. Over time, the coyote's network

59

was dismantled, and his lookouts were either arrested or scattered.

Agents filed charges of human smuggling and conspiracy against the coyote. During questioning, the female agent asked him why he did it, knowing the danger and the consequences. The coyote shrugged, his voice hollow, "People need to get across. I tried to do it without hurting anyone."

Long after his capture, the coyote's story echoed through the valleys and towns of the borderlands. Some said he took advantage of the vulnerable; others argued he offered hope in a world with too few options.

For the twelve passengers, life continued. Some were released to relatives in the U.S., while others returned to their countries; dreams deferred, but not extinguished. For the female agent, there were more cases, more choices, each weighed against the backdrop of her own family's journey decades earlier.

The border has always been both a barrier and a bridge. The stories full of hope, risk, and consequence kept unfolding with each crossing.

CHAPTER 10

Covert Operations

At times, conducting undercover work was essential to establishing a criminal case. Agents in this role hold a crucial position in law enforcement, operating at the edge between official authority and the criminal underworld. We often had to put ourselves in danger to pursue justice.

Our responsibilities require bravery, flexibility, and confidentiality. Utilizing secrecy and deception, we infiltrate criminal organizations, gather intelligence, and contribute to the dismantling of illicit networks that pose a threat to society.

A little fact: The history and development of undercover operations date back centuries, rooted in early espionage and intelligence efforts during wars and periods of political upheaval. In the United States, undercover work gained prominence in the late 1800s and early 1900s, particularly during periods of civil unrest and the rise of organized crime. Agencies started deploying agents into covert roles to keep watch on radical groups, bootleggers, and mobsters.

During the prohibition and gangster era, undercover agents tirelessly aimed to apprehend notorious criminals like Al Capone. The innovative methods they created then laid the foundation for modern undercover operations, which now leverage advanced technology and psychological knowledge to enhance effectiveness and safety.

Working undercover, we undertook various missions that required careful planning and execution. Initially, we had to build credibility and gain access within criminal groups, a process that can take months or even years to accomplish.

Next, we carefully gathered valuable information on criminal activities, organizational setup, and any plans the organization might have had. Collecting these details will help us achieve our goal of bringing criminals to justice through arrest and prosecution.

Whenever we can, we actively work to prevent terrorist plots, drug trafficking, human trafficking, and other crimes. It's all about staying a step ahead to build a safer and more secure world for us all.

We had to maintain our cover and identities, which often included fabricated backgrounds, employment histories, and even families. We convincingly play our roles, sometimes participating in criminal acts to avoid suspicion, though constantly carefully monitored to remain within legal and ethical boundaries.

Selection and Training

Not all agents are fit for undercover operations. They must pass comprehensive psychological and physical screenings to evaluate traits like resilience, adaptability, and emotional steadiness. Quick thinking, improvisation skills, and remaining calm under pressure are essential qualities.

Training for the undercover role includes role-playing and scenario simulations, enabling agents to practice encounters they might face in the field. This encompasses skills such as discreetly observing suspects and understanding the legal and ethical boundaries of their actions.

Additionally, there are helpful psychological resilience learning techniques that can assist you in managing stress, feelings of isolation, and moral uncertainty. These techniques also help you develop practical communication skills, including mastering both verbal and nonverbal ways of connecting with others.

Working undercover was a tense and dangerous experience, filled with risk and mental stress. Some of the biggest challenges included the threat to personal safety. We faced violence if our cover was exposed or if we failed to meet the expectations of criminal associates. The mental pressure of living a double life can lead to anxiety, depression, and confusion about one's identity.

Isolation significantly impacts social connections, leading to emotional estrangement and potential deterioration of personal relationships. Ethical dilemmas arose when individuals occasionally engaged in or observed criminal activities, prompting critical questions concerning morality and legality.

Some operations were a long-term commitment where operations could last years, demanding sustained deception and vigilance. This was where a sound support system within the agency, such as counseling, peer networks, and periodic reassignment, was crucial in helping us navigate these challenges and return to normal.

Our undercover work had resulted in the dismantling of major criminal organizations and the capture of high-profile fugitives. Operations, along with various joint-agency stings targeting drug, weapons, and trafficking rings, have influenced legal precedent and public awareness.

Beyond arrests and convictions, we often played a key role in shaping legislative change. By detailing the methods and scope of criminal enterprises, this informed policymakers and prompted reforms to close loopholes and increase penalties for organized crime.

Of course, with great power comes great responsibility. Federal undercover operations are subject to strict oversight to ensure agents do not cross legal boundaries or violate civil rights.

Internal review boards, independent commissions, and federal courts regularly evaluate undercover tactics to balance the need for secrecy with the importance of accountability.

Some agencies implement "rules of engagement," which are strict protocol that governs agents' behavior in the field. These rules were designed to minimize harm, ensure due process, and uphold the integrity of law enforcement.

Meeting Informants in Clandestine Places

I want to quickly talk about the art and subtlety of having secret encounters and meetings.

In the dark corners of the world where certainty is rare and trust takes time to build, special agents gather discreetly. Their secret meetings happen away from public eye, using whispered codes, subtle signals, and hidden agendas. These covert gatherings are not just fictional; across many regions and eras, they are fundamental to intelligence, diplomacy, and occasionally the delicate balance between peace and chaos.

The concept of gathering information through secret meetings has existed since ancient times. Early civilizations employed messengers and spies to share secrets in places like temples, markets, or under moonlit skies at crossroads.

During the European Renaissance, secret notes were passed

in candlelit taverns, and during wartime, encrypted codes and signals conveyed vital intelligence. While techniques have improved over time, the main objective remains unchanged: to exchange sensitive information discreetly and prevent unauthorized access.

Why Clandestine Places?

The term "clandestine" evokes scenes of shadowy alleys, rain-soaked streets, and quiet hotel rooms. For agents, gathering in these locations is not just romantic but essential for survival and strategic reasons. Maintaining secrecy allows information to be exchanged securely, identities to stay safe, and missions to continue smoothly without interference.

These locations are carefully chosen, taking into account escape routes, surveillance risks, and the local environment's rhythm. The architecture of a clandestine meeting is as much psychological as it is physical, requiring a balance between concealment and accessibility. Sometimes, the best hiding place is in plain sight, amidst the everyday bustle—a crowded market, a noisy café, or a busy train station.

Clandestine locations are chosen for their ability to provide privacy, plausible deniability, and environmental control. The goal is to hide not only the meeting's content but also the very fact that a meeting is happening. Parks at dusk, empty parking garages, quiet cafés with back entrances, and busy markets are common venues. Clandestine places must strike a balance between being inconspicuous—blending into everyday life—and offering escape routes and ways to detect surveillance.

Privacy is vital for protecting conversations from eavesdroppers, whether physical or electronic. Deniability is also essential, as it allows both parties to deny involvement if caught plausibly. Additionally, control features let the initiator manage access, oversee the environment, and retreat if necessary.

For special agents, clandestine meetings are not only a test of their skills but also an actual test of nerves. The suspense of the unknown—the risk of surveillance, betrayal, or ambush—calls for a calm and composed mind. Agents are taught to be attentive to subtle changes around them, trust their instincts without becoming paranoid, and share vital details even when words are hard to find.

Trust in clandestine work is a rare commodity. Agents may have worked together for years yet know little about one another's actual lives. The necessity of secrecy breeds both camaraderie and caution. Rituals emerge—shared signals, coded phrases, even particular ways of greeting—that reinforce trust while maintaining operational distance.

Secrecy carries risks. Secret meetings, if found out, can result in arrest, exposure, or violence. Agents must constantly balance the benefits of direct contact with the dangers of surveillance and betrayal. Protocols for planning and conducting these meetings are strict: they include multiple backup plans, contingency layers, and emergency signals.

Behind the shadowy work of clandestine agents lies a complex web of ethical questions. What lines are crossed in the pursuit of information? How does the constant need for secrecy affect the agents' lives, relationships, and sense of self? Many operatives speak of the isolation that comes with the work, the burden of secrets carried in silence.

For some, the challenge is energizing because they understand that their concealed actions can help maintain peace, avoid conflicts, or shield innocent lives. The secret meeting serves not just as a strategic move but also as a representation of the moral complexities involved in intelligence activities.

Sometimes, simple mistakes such as a misread signal or an unexpected observer can unravel months of careful planning. The stakes are high, for the agents themselves and, often, for the broader strategic objectives they serve.

Special agents meeting in clandestine places embody the intersection of art and necessity in the world of intelligence. Their work, shrouded in secrecy and fraught with risk, is vital to the preservation of security, the advancement of diplomacy, and the unfolding of history itself. Beneath the surface glamour and danger lies a world built on trust, ingenuity, and the relentless quest for answers in the face of the unknown.

As the world changes, so do the ways and meanings of secret meetings. In every dark alley and hidden room, the timeless dance goes on as proof of humanity's lasting ability for secrecy, strategy, and survival.

To keep secrets, one must stay constantly alert to those trying to uncover them. Special agents train to detect surveillance, shake tails, and prevent infiltration. Sometimes, the most important secret is the agent's very presence or absence in a specific place at a specific time.

In a world where information is power, the delicate skill of keeping secrets has been refined over centuries, shaped through times of conflict, and constantly evolving. It remains one of humanity's most meaningful pursuits. The special agent, quiet and unnoticed, symbolizes this timeless tradition—a living reminder of the strength found in silence and what is left unsaid.

In the end, you met with no one at a location that doesn't exist and obtained no information that you are aware of. What?

Now, if you are totally confused, I did my job.

CHAPTER 11

Combating Domestic Terrorism

Domestic terrorism refers to acts of violence or threats of violence committed by individuals or groups within the U.S., intended to intimidate or coerce a civilian population or influence government policy, without foreign direction.

The Federal Bureau of Investigation (FBI) is the lead federal agency tasked with investigating and addressing domestic terrorism. ICE agents, as an arm of DHS, may support these agencies in certain circumstances, especially if there are cross-border elements or violations of immigration law.

Although ICE does not lead domestic terrorism investigations, its agents may become involved in cases under certain conditions. If a suspect in a domestic terrorism case is a non-citizen and subject to immigration enforcement actions, ICE may investigate and potentially detain or deport that individual.

If terrorist activities include cross-border crimes like smuggling weapons, people, or money into or out of the U.S. for terrorism, ICE's HSI agents are involved in investigating these cases.

ICE agents assist in joint task forces, such as the Joint Terrorism Task Force (JTTF), which bring together multiple agencies to address complex terrorism threats.

In these situations, ICE agents lend their expertise in immigration, customs, and international crime.

Domestic terrorism represents a significant security threat today. Unlike external terrorism, which originates outside a country, domestic terrorism is conducted by individuals or groups within the nation. These perpetrators are driven by various beliefs such as religious extremism, political radicalism, racial supremacy, and anti-government sentiments.

Special agents receive specialized training to collaborate with other federal, state, and local agencies. Task forces are established to investigate, prevent, and respond to acts of domestic terrorism. The work is both complex and essential, aiming to protect the public while safeguarding civil liberties.

Common examples of domestic terrorism include attacks on places of worship motivated by hatred or bigotry, bombings or threats against government buildings, assassinations or kidnappings for political motives, and mass shootings driven by ideological extremism.

Agents investigating domestic terrorism operate at the intersection of law enforcement, intelligence, and community engagement. Their role requires not only technical expertise but also a deep understanding of social dynamics, political environments, and cultural influences.

Agents depend largely on intelligence gathered from human sources, surveillance, cyber monitoring, and open-source platforms. They examine patterns in behavior, communications, and financial transactions to map networks and spot threats.

Strict legal frameworks govern domestic investigations to protect civil liberties. Agents must carefully balance the need to prevent violence with the rights guaranteed by the Constitution and legal statutes.

Lone actors, often called "lone wolves," are individuals who carry out attacks independently, without support from organized groups. Agents use behavioral analysis, public tips, and digital surveillance to detect and prevent these threats. For instance, community vigilance, paired with swift police intervention, has successfully prevented multiple planned attacks in recent years.

Investigations focus on organized extremist groups that are involved in planning or encouraging violence. Over recent years, we've seen an increase in militia movements, hate groups, and radicalized cells. By sending in undercover agents or recruiting informants, agencies have successfully gathered evidence, disrupted their funding, and made arrests of essential members.

Technological progress has revolutionized investigation methods. Agents now rely on data analytics, facial recognition, and AI to swiftly handle large volumes of information. Digital forensics teams examine seized devices, while cyber units monitor online activities.

Agents investigating domestic terrorism play a crucial role in safeguarding safety, freedom, and democratic principles. Through careful investigation, legal precision, technological advancements, and community engagement, they act as a barrier against violence and division. Their continuous efforts, along with societal cooperation, are vital to addressing the changing threats of domestic terrorism.

ICE agents play a vital role in protecting the United States from cross-border crime, enforcing immigration laws, and supporting broader homeland security goals.

While ICE may occasionally become involved in investigations that touch on domestic terrorism, especially when international or immigration aspects are present, the primary responsibility for investigating and prosecuting domestic terrorism belongs to agencies such as the FBI, ATF, and DOJ.

Understanding the division of duties among federal law enforcement agencies is essential for comprehending how the U.S. government responds to the evolving threat of domestic terrorism.

CHAPTER 12

Undercover and Family Life

To lead a double life is to walk a tightrope stretched between two worlds: the shadowy corridors of espionage and the warm, light-filled rooms of home. Working undercover, every day is a performance, every relationship a calculated risk, every moment a test of loyalty not only to the mission, but also to the people we hold most dear. Yet, behind the mystique and adrenaline of clandestine work, we often grapple with the most human of challenges: nurturing family life while keeping secrets that must never be revealed.

We had to work in environments fraught with uncertainty and danger. The assignments required us to assume false identities, infiltrate criminal organizations, or cultivate relationships with targets. The work was as much psychological as it was strategic, demanding adaptability, emotional resilience, and unwavering discretion. The stakes were high; one misstep could imperil not only me, but potentially my loved ones. The necessity of secrecy pervades every aspect of life, extending from classified operations to mundane family moments. Cell phones may be left behind, stories may be abridged, and specific topics may be forever off-limits at the dinner table.

The Psychological Toll

The burden of living a lie, even temporarily, can be profound. Undercover, I constantly monitored my behavior, words, and emotions, lest I inadvertently betray my true identity. This vigilance does not abate when I return home; the habit of caution can bleed into personal interactions, creating distance and suspicion even among those closest to me.

At times, I spent weeks or months embedded in a false existence, cultivating trust among strangers while withholding the truth from family. The psychological cost manifested as anxiety, guilt, and alienation, complicating efforts to maintain genuine intimacy at home.

Family life thrives on communication, trust, and shared experiences. Being undercover, these elements were often restricted by the demands of the job. Linda was aware of the general nature of my work, but not the specifics. Sometimes, cover stories were devised to explain lengthy absences, sudden schedule changes, or emotional withdrawal.

Life After Undercover Work

Undercover work is often romanticized in books, movies, and popular culture. The excitement of living with a secret identity, gathering intelligence, and sneaking into secret organizations is appealing. But what happens after the mission is over? The life of an agent after undercover work is complicated, involving psychological adjustments, personal reinvention, and the challenge of fitting back into the world they once knew—one filled with secrets and shaped by experiences few others will understand.

One of the biggest challenges after working undercover was regaining our true identity. During deep cover, we often adopted new names, backgrounds, and even belief systems, sometimes for months or years. The daily act of living a lie, no matter how noble the cause, can wear down the lines between the assumed persona and the real self.

Upon returning to our true identity, we at times experienced a sense of dislocation or confusion. The world we left behind felt a little foreign, and our own reflection unfamiliar. The process of disentangling our genuine self from our undercover role required time, support, and introspection. It often involved therapy, debriefings, and a gradual reintroduction to the rhythms of ordinary life.

I knew of former agents who struggled with memories that linger, flashbacks, dreams, or even a subtle longing for the adrenaline-charged days of covert existence.

Most often, after an undercover mission, some agents are reassigned to desk jobs, training roles, or investigative units. The transition from the unpredictable, high-stakes environment of undercover work, where every day brought new surprises and decisions had immediate consequences, to a more routine professional setting can be jarring. Some agents welcome the normalcy and stability, while others struggle to adapt to a pace that feels slow or lacks purpose.

Maintaining secrecy about the specifics of undercover operations, sometimes for the rest of your life, can limit your ability to discuss achievements and advocate for promotions or new opportunities. The confidential nature of our work meant that significant accomplishments often went unrecognized, and blending back into a larger organization felt isolating.

Undercover assignments often require us to distance ourselves from our families, keep secrets, and occasionally invent explanations for our absence or actions. When we return from this period of enforced separation, we might discover that relationships have changed, trust has been challenged, and emotional bonds need to be reestablished.

Spouses and children may have grown accustomed to independence, or may struggle to understand the reasons behind our secrecy and emotional distance. Re-establishing intimacy and communication can take time, patience, and honesty.

Even after an undercover assignment has ended, some agents may continue to face threats from individuals or organizations they helped investigate or disrupt. In some cases, the agent's identity was compromised, requiring ongoing vigilance and, in rare instances, relocation or a new identity.

The life of an agent after undercover work is a tapestry woven from threads of triumph, struggle, loss, and renewal. It involves rediscovering oneself, rebuilding relationships, and finding one's place in a world that may feel forever changed. While the scars of secrecy may remain, so does the strength gained from overcoming adversity. In the end, life after undercover work is not just a return, but a transformation, a tribute to the courage and resilience of those who have walked the line between shadow and light.

The Spouse's Perspective

Linda bore a unique burden because she had to navigate a relationship marked by ambiguity and, at times, deception. The absence of clear information could lead to insecurity, frustration, and concern for my safety. I know she noticed behavioral changes: emotional exhaustion, irritability, and avoidance of specific topics. Just the knowledge of my work caused her chronic anxiety, but she demonstrated remarkable resilience. I think she learned to read between the lines, to offer support without prying, and to cherish the moments of connection that remain untouched by secrecy.

Being an undercover agent meant living a life of paradox, guarding secrets while longing for openness, facing danger yet cherishing safety, forging relationships on both sides of the divide. For those of us who chose this path, the demands are enormous, but so too are the rewards: the opportunity to serve a greater cause, to protect society, and to return home, at last, to the embrace of family.

Linda's journey involved sacrifices, but through strength, adaptability, and unwavering love, she found ways to endure and, in moments of grace, to truly thrive. In the end, it was her quiet courage that sustained me, both in the shadows and in the light of home.

CHAPTER 13

The Role of Compassion

For many, the title "Special Agent" evokes images of sharp suits, fast-paced chases, and unwavering determination in the face of danger. As agents, our mission was to uphold the law and keep the public safe, guided by discipline and professionalism. But beyond the badge and the bravado, there's an essential quality that truly makes you an agent: compassion. Combining sharp investigative skills with genuine empathy not only boosts your effectiveness but also helps ensure that justice is delivered with respect and human dignity.

Special Agents occupy a unique place in law enforcement and intelligence communities. Our work spans a spectrum, everything from counterterrorism and organized crime investigations to cyber threats and missing persons cases. The pressure is immense; the stakes are high. Agents must make decisions quickly, often in rapidly shifting circumstances, and frequently bear the responsibility for life-or-death outcomes.

Yet, our work was not done in a vacuum. Every case, every operation involved people, victims, witnesses, suspects, and the broader communities impacted by crime and crisis. The temptation to become hardened by the intensity of the job was ever-present, but it was precisely here that compassion became essential.

Compassion goes beyond just feeling sentimental. It's a heartfelt understanding of others' pain, combined with a sincere wish to help ease that suffering. In law enforcement, showing compassion means listening with an open mind, treating everyone with kindness and respect, regardless of the situation, and striving for results that heal and restore rather than punish.

For me, compassion was a strength, not a weakness. It shaped how I engaged with crime victims, ensuring their voices were heard and their trauma validated. It also influenced how I interacted with suspects, many of whom might be caught in cycles of abuse, addiction, or desperation. Compassion motivated me to consider what was morally right beyond just following the law.

When interviewing a crime victim, my approach could make all the difference. A compassionate agent creates a safe space, allowing individuals to share their stories without fear, shame, or intimidation. This not only aided the investigation by yielding more accurate and complete accounts, but also helped victims begin the process of healing.

Compassion did not mean excusing unlawful behavior, but it did mean recognizing the humanity in every individual. Agents who treat suspects with dignity are more likely to gain cooperation, reduce hostility, and avoid unnecessary escalation.

A Special Agent's role was often isolating and emotionally demanding. Showing compassion toward colleagues fosters trust, promotes mutual support, and strengthens resilience within teams. When agents support each other both professionally and personally, it benefits the entire organization.

Despite its importance, maintaining compassion was not always an easy task. Special Agents were exposed to some of the harshest realities of human behavior—violence, deception, exploitation. The risk of emotional burnout, cynicism, and detachment was very real.

To address this, the agency prioritizes the mental health and well-being of agents. Regular training in emotional intelligence, access to counseling services, and strong peer support networks were vital. We also had to develop tools for self-care: mindfulness, exercise, healthy boundaries, and the willingness to seek help when needed.

The practice of compassion was deeply intertwined with ethical conduct. Special Agents wield extraordinary powers, including the authority to detain, interrogate, and, if necessary, use force. Compassion acted as a safeguard against abuses of power. It reminded agents to respect rights, to weigh consequences, and to remember that the end does not always justify the means.

Moreover, compassion pushes agents to be self-critical, to question their own biases, and to confront the systemic injustices that may exist within the institutions they serve. It encourages transparency and accountability, helping to build public trust in law enforcement agencies.

Balancing Compassion with Duty

The challenge lies in striking a balance between compassion and the harsh realities of law enforcement. There are moments when agents must act decisively to protect others, even when doing so causes pain or discomfort. Compassion does not mean indecision; it means choosing the most humane path available, even when the choices are difficult.

Agents must learn to set boundaries, differentiate between empathy and over-identification, and maintain professional detachment when necessary. The aim is not to be overwhelmed by others' suffering but to be inspired by it, acting with purpose, integrity, and compassion.

As an agent, I held a role steeped in responsibility, one that required an unwavering commitment to the rule of law. Yet, it was compassion, the ability to see, feel, and respond to the suffering of others, that elevated the work from mere enforcement to genuine service.

In the pursuit of justice, compassion was not only desirable but essential. It was the quiet force that transformed lives, strengthened communities, and upheld the profession's noblest ideals.

CHAPTER 14

Asset Forfeiture Group, Washington, DC

On April 1, 2007, while supervising the CAP unit, I was assigned to the headquarters of ICE in Washington, D.C., where I was detailed to serve in the Asset Forfeiture Unit (AFU). This division at headquarters was understaffed, leading to supervisory agents from the field being assigned to support the office during a ninety-day detail.

The AFU was dedicated to identifying, seizing, and forfeiting assets derived from criminal activity, including transnational organized crime, drug trafficking, human smuggling, financial fraud, and other illicit enterprises.

The AFU special agents played a significant role in disrupting criminal operations and recovering the proceeds of a crime. They also assisted the field offices in tracing the proceeds of a crime, identifying assets acquired with illicit funds, and initiating legal proceedings to seize and forfeit those assets through civil and criminal forfeiture actions. When you can deprive criminals of their financial resources, it disrupts their entire operation.

Asset forfeiture enables the federal government to seize property associated with a crime. This can include both the tools used to commit a crime and the proceeds.

Civil forfeiture and criminal forfeiture effectively accomplish the same goals; however, criminal forfeiture is contingent upon a conviction being obtained. As part of sentencing, the court may order the defendant to forfeit certain assets believed to be related to the crime.

AFU agents also conducted financial investigations into the activities of criminal organizations, utilizing forensic accounting techniques, financial analysis tools, and investigative methods to uncover evidence of asset concealment, money laundering, and other financial crimes.

We worked closely with other law enforcement agencies, financial institutions, regulatory bodies, and international partners to share information, coordinate operations, and maximize the impact of asset forfeiture efforts.

I reported directly to the Unit Chief of the AFU. I was assigned to oversee the twenty-four investigative field offices across the U.S. and assist in seizing assets obtained during criminal investigations.

The AFU agents employed a range of enforcement strategies to identify and seize assets derived from crime, including real estate, vehicles, cash, bank accounts, and other valuable property. We followed the money trail, traced the flow of funds, and located assets used to facilitate or finance crime. We also executed search warrants, issued subpoenas and court orders, and coordinated asset seizure and forfeiture proceedings with federal prosecutors and law enforcement partners.

This detail kept me very busy. I worked all day long on weekdays, starting work at 7:30 a.m. and working until 6 or 7 p.m. every night. The hours in AFU were long and tedious, but I had weekends off and tried to make the most of them to have fun.

Working in DC was a fun assignment, too. There was a wealth of history to be found, and visiting the Smithsonian was free of charge. I would go on Saturdays and spend the entire day going through the museums. However, on many weekends, I would be so tired that sleeping in was a necessity. It was nice to sleep in as long as you wanted. I needed it too. The weeks were long and very busy, with a lot of traveling.

One day, while at work, the Unit Chief called me into his office and informed me that a Section Chief position was available for the office. He asked me if I was interested in the position, and he printed a copy of the announcement for me. When he handed it to me, he said, "It's yours if you want it."

I took the announcement and told him I had to think about it and speak with Linda. This would be a significant move for us, so it was only fair to discuss it with Linda before giving my answer.

I later spoke with Linda about the position and explained that it would give me a substantial raise and upgrade, leading to future advancements. After speaking with Linda, she agreed, so I submitted my application for the position and notified the Unit Chief.

On April 20, 2007, the Unit Chief called me into his office and said, "Congratulations, you have the position." I officially accepted a three-year term with the possibility of two one-year extensions, making it a five-year assignment after I return to the field to work.

I later returned to the New Orleans investigations office and informed my unit that I would be transferring to the AFU in DC. Everyone in the unit was sad to see me leave, but they understood my reasons, and several agents even tried to follow me to DC.

It took a few months for me to receive my official transfer orders, but that was fine because I had a lot to do before leaving for DC, cleaning up case work, and making arrangements with Linda for the move.

Linda and I discussed our options, and we decided that she would stay in Amite while I worked in DC. I knew I would be traveling frequently in my new position, and I learned that I could plan my travels to pass through New Orleans and stay for a few days with Linda before returning to DC. Also, Linda would fly Delta Airlines on a straight flight from New Orleans to DC, and with my air miles building up, it would not cost her anything to travel to see me.

As it turned out, I spent months traveling three weeks at a time, flying from one city to another. We didn't see the need for Linda to spend weeks at a time in DC by herself.

Working in New Orleans was enjoyable, and I learned a great deal while supervising some exceptional agents. Working in DC at AFU will provide terrific opportunities for advancement and learning new aspects of the job.

CHAPTER 15

Section Chief

On August 1, 2007, I returned to ICE Headquarters in Washington, D.C., as the Section Chief of the Asset Forfeiture Unit (AFU).

As Section Chief, I supervised a staff of ICE Special Agents, Program Managers (PM), Administrative Personnel, and government contractors. I also managed a multi-million-dollar budget from the U.S. Treasury Forfeiture Fund to support ICE's ongoing national forfeitures and investigative programs. I also oversaw the seizures from the twenty-four ICE investigative field offices.

Asset forfeiture serves as a vital tool in U.S. law enforcement, enabling the disruption and dismantling of criminal organizations by seizing their illicit gains. U.S. Immigration and Customs Enforcement (ICE), especially Homeland Security Investigations (HSI), plays a key role in these efforts, investigating various crimes such as drug trafficking and immigration fraud.

Asset forfeiture refers to the legal process by which law enforcement agencies seize assets derived from or used to facilitate criminal activity. In the United States, this practice is grounded in both civil and criminal law.

Civil Asset Forfeiture is a proceeding brought against the property itself, rather than the individual. The burden of proof is typically lower, requiring only a preponderance of the evidence to establish a connection to criminal activity.

Criminal Asset Forfeiture occurs after a criminal conviction, with assets seized as part of the sentencing process. The government must prove beyond a reasonable doubt that the assets are connected to the convicted offense.

ICE agents may pursue either route, depending on the facts, the urgency of the case, and the likelihood of a successful criminal prosecution.

During my time with Asset Forfeiture, we explored a wide range of criminal activities. These included drug trafficking and smuggling, human trafficking and slavery, immigration-related fraud, money laundering and financial crimes, intellectual property theft, and activities by transnational gangs and organized crime groups. We worked diligently to uncover and understand these complex issues, always aiming to contribute to a safer community.

Asset forfeiture played a crucial role in these investigations, as eliminating the financial incentives and infrastructure behind criminal networks is often more effective than prosecuting individuals alone.

Initiating an Investigation

Typically, agents begin by identifying suspects and entities that may have assets associated with illegal activities. They gather intelligence from multiple sources, including ongoing undercover operations, financial monitoring, suspicious activity reports, tips from the public or confidential informants, collaborations with domestic and international partners, and data collected from immigration enforcement actions.

After identifying potential assets, agents collaborate with financial analysts and legal counsel to trace the suspected flow of criminal proceeds and decide on the best course of action.

Agents often work closely with various federal agencies, including the FBI, DEA, IRS, and U.S. Marshals, as well as state and local law enforcement. Together, they collaborate through task forces or joint operations, which help them share information, skills, and resources effectively.

Investigative Techniques

Asset forfeiture investigations require a blend of traditional investigative work and advanced financial analysis. Key activities include tracing the ownership and movement of assets through complex corporate structures or offshore accounts, as well as conducting surveillance on targets and their associates.

Agents may also execute search and seizure warrants for properties, bank accounts, vehicles, and luxury goods while analyzing tax filings, wire transfers, and other financial records.

Then, once all information is collected, the interviews with witnesses, informants, or cooperating defendants will begin.

Agents, particularly those with specialized training in financial crimes, utilize advanced technologies to link the connections within illicit networks.

Seizure and Forfeiture Process

Once enough evidence is established, the process of seizing assets can be swift. A seizure can be physical or legal control taken over the asset. Agents may seize cash, real estate, vehicles, bank accounts, and even digital assets, such as cryptocurrencies.

ICE notifies the owners and any interested parties, allowing them to contest the seizure in court. If uncontested, the asset may be administratively forfeited. If contested, the government must prevail in federal court to retain the asset.

After the seizure, assets may be sold, repurposed for law enforcement use, or returned to victims as some form of restitution.

ICE and the Department of Homeland Security (DHS) have

implemented internal policies to mitigate risks and ensure the integrity of asset forfeiture cases. In addition, congressional oversight and external advocacy groups continue to monitor and critique ICE's forfeiture practices.

Asset forfeiture, when applied judiciously, can disrupt criminal organizations, return funds to victims, and strengthen the enforcement of immigration and customs laws. However, the process must strike a balance between law enforcement effectiveness and the preservation of civil liberties and due process. Agents are continually trained to navigate this delicate balance, ensuring that justice is served without overstepping their authority.

Agents involved in asset forfeiture cases work at the crossroads of finance, law, and national security. Their responsibilities are complex and sometimes contentious, demanding a sophisticated grasp of legal principles, investigative methods, and ethical considerations. As legislation and public opinion evolve, ICE continually adapts its strategies for pursuing illicit assets, striving to strike a balance between security and justice.

When the investigative field offices seized items during their investigations, such as houses, cars, assorted property, animals (including horses or cattle), and money, we at AFU Headquarters would assume total control and management of those assets.

Once all the items were collected, I would calculate the monetary value and then distribute the proceeds among all the participating agencies involved in the case. This money was essential to the departments involved because it would help them buy equipment for their agency.

One of the most essential functions I had as Section Chief was to ensure that seizures were both fiscally responsible and legally sound, able to withstand public and legal scrutiny. We had to ensure that the investigative field offices gathered evidence during the investigation and planned for the legal and logistical aspects of seizures and forfeitures. We considered the economic impact of each seizure, including the cost of management, storage, depreciation, and disposal of the seized property.

An example would be seizing a vehicle worth more than its value. In this case, seizing the vehicle would not be feasible because it would incur a cost to the government, namely the cost of paying off the vehicle.

Field Office Inspections

AFU also conducted inspections at ICE field offices during investigations into asset seizure and forfeiture. These inspections were crucial for identifying and confiscating assets linked to criminal activity, as well as for ensuring that field offices complied with federal laws and ICE regulations.

It also contributed to safeguarding the integrity of the asset forfeiture process by verifying that seized assets were meticulously documented, securely stored, and properly managed. Additionally, this process ensured adherence to all legal procedures, thereby preventing potential legal challenges.

As the Section Chief, I facilitated the execution of inspections within twenty-four field offices and their respective suboffices throughout the United States, Hawaii, Guam, Puerto Rico, and the U.S. Virgin Islands. The inspection process encompassed an examination of the seized property rooms, which housed evidence and other confiscated items. We evaluated the procedures for collecting, processing, and storing evidence and seized property.

Seized property storage rooms needed to meet specific size standards and be equipped with locks, sensors, and cameras to ensure everything remained secure and safe. All items stored there had to be carefully documented and managed in accordance with ICE policies and procedures, ensuring that everything was properly maintained.

The office inspections typically took a day or less, depending on the office size and the quantity of stored property; larger offices sometimes required three days or more.

Traveling to these offices was not an undesirable duty;

however, it required traveling three weeks each month. I have traveled extensively across the United States, including multiple visits to Guam and Hawaii, where I have reviewed office procedures and provided assistance in investigations.

I have also traveled extensively across the United States, visiting prominent destinations such as Las Vegas, Yellowstone National Park, Long Beach, California, Nogales, New Mexico, Mount Rushmore, the Liberty Bell, Seattle, and sixty-six other cities.

Federal Air Marshal (FAM)

Before September 11, 2001, while on official government duty with service weapons, we checked in at the airline counter, presented our credentials, and completed the required paperwork to fly armed. After check-in, we proceeded past the TSA security checkpoint to the local police station at the airport, where we signed the logbook with an officer. We then boarded our flight at the designated gate. Upon arrival, we submitted a copy of our paperwork to the airline at the entrance, confirming that we were law enforcement officers (LEOs) carrying arms.

Following the September 11, 2001, attacks, airlines underwent minor modifications with the establishment of the U.S. Federal Air Marshals (FAM). This newly formed agency was designated to accompany flights to various destinations as a preventive measure.

The FAM is a federal law enforcement agency managed by the Transportation Security Administration (TSA), a component of the U.S. Department of Homeland Security (DHS). Due to their responsibilities, FAMs frequently travel and must be highly proficient marksmen.

As LEOs, we had to stay incognito and blend in with other passengers. The only times we should intervene are if a passenger tries to hijack the plane, open an aircraft door, or physically threaten another passenger or flight attendant.

In July 2008, I was asked by the Deputy Assistant Director of the Office of Professional Responsibility (OPR) to consider a transfer to the OPR Special Investigations Unit (SIU) in Alexandria, Virginia. Remember, OPR is the internal affairs division for ICE.

After careful consideration and, of course, consulting with Linda, I decided to transfer from Asset Forfeiture and return to investigations in OPR.

Before making my decision, I thoroughly researched the role, including its responsibilities, required qualifications, and potential challenges.

I understood that internal affairs investigators are responsible for examining breaches of agency policies, misuse of public positions, and criminal activities involving department staff. The role demanded a strong sense of integrity, professionalism, and skill. Additionally, I was required to undergo an extensive background check comparable to that of prospective employees.

I realized that the role required closely analyzing the actions and words of others, which can sometimes be a challenging task. However, I also understood the purpose of the OPR.

Its goal is to safeguard, not to antagonize, and to promote respect and collaboration among all government staff.

CHAPTER 16

Office of Professional Responsibility (OPR)

Washington, DC

In September 2008, I received my orders transferring me from the Asset Forfeiture Unit to the OPR as a Special Agent (SA) assigned to the Special Investigations Unit (SIU) in Alexandria, Virginia. As I previously mentioned, OPR is the internal affairs division for DHS/ICE.

On October 12, 2008, I began my first day at the SIU. In my early days, I focused on understanding the roles of the agents. I had a broad understanding, but never fully comprehended all of OPR's duties and responsibilities.

I soon discovered that the OPR SIU was deeply involved in coordinating and conducting intricate and sensitive investigations. These investigations often focus on alleged misconduct, criminal activities, and corruption involving Department of Homeland Security (DHS) employees and their associated entities.

The path to working in OPR involved accumulating relevant law enforcement experience, investigative skills, and a reputation for professionalism and integrity. I had specialized training in investigations, forensic analysis, and interviewing techniques.

Securing a recommendation to work in OPR was highly competitive and required a demonstrated history of ethical conduct, discretion, and investigative acumen. I underwent intensive background checks to ensure my suitability.

Once established in OPR, I was expected to participate in regular training to stay up-to-date with evolving legal standards, investigative techniques, and best practices in oversight and anti-corruption efforts.

The Department of Homeland Security, ICE, plays a crucial role in the United States, working tirelessly to catch undocumented individuals, dismantle trafficking networks, and oversee the legal movement of goods and people. OPR functions as the agency's dedicated internal watchdog, committed to investigating reports of misconduct, corruption, abuse of power, or policy violations by ICE staff. OPR's primary goal is to uphold the highest standards of integrity and accountability, ensuring all agents and employees follow ethical and legal guidelines.

As an OPR agent, I was tasked with a range of sensitive and often confidential duties, including investigating allegations of misconduct against ICE employees. These allegations encompassed accusations of unlawful conduct, excessive use of force, discrimination, harassment, corruption, or any behavior that undermines public trust. I conducted interviews of witnesses and gathered evidence.

Critical to my investigation, I interviewed ICE personnel, external witnesses, and, when necessary, individuals held in ICE custody. I collected, preserved, and analyzed physical and digital evidence, ensuring proper chain of custody and adherence to legal protocols.

After each case, I generated detailed reports for ICE leadership and, in some instances, for oversight bodies, which helped inform policy decisions and demonstrate the agency's commitment to accountability.

Our team of agents was diverse, conducting thorough, unbiased, and professional investigations to support our overall mission. We focused on accountability, professionalism, and integrity.

We often handle assignments that involve gathering and analyzing essential information, facts, evidence, and intelligence from various sources. These include law enforcement and government databases, crime scene and use-of-force incident reports, as well as detailed interviews with involved employees and witnesses. Many of our cases involve investigating incidents where force was used, whether lethal or non-lethal, encompassing everything from responding to incidents to processing the scene and preparing detailed investigative reports.

We fully utilized the agency's resources to support investigations into criminal corruption, employee misconduct, counterterrorism, and counterintelligence, all of which directly impact our national security and the integrity of our agency. We prepared detailed reports of our investigations and were glad to testify in court or other proceedings to share our findings.

We also scrutinized key interregional issues of national or international importance. This entailed analyzing individuals, enterprises, employees, and criminal organizations that constitute a substantial threat to the national security of the United States through corruption or attempted corrupt activities, including foreign intelligence agencies and terrorist groups targeting federal personnel.

The SIU office was located in Arlington, VA. On occasion, I was assigned to investigate allegations involving DHS senior executives and other sensitive, high-profile investigative matters. The SIU investigations often involve critical incidents and significant cases likely to generate media, congressional, or departmental interest, both domestically and internationally.

Our unit Chief was strict during investigations, but he also enjoyed playing pranks. It took me some time to get to know him and to figure out when he was serious or joking. When it came to investigative work and questions about cases, he was focused and firm, with no hesitation or doubt.

During my time at SIU, the Unit Chief and I became close friends, and we stayed in touch until he retired and left government service.

Reviewing allegations

When the SIU received an allegation, the first step was to conduct an initial review of the allegation to decide if further investigation was necessary. This decision was based on several factors, including the nature of the allegation, its credibility, specificity, likelihood of verification, and, of course, the source.

Most allegations received were found not to warrant further review because, for example, the complaint appeared without merit, was outside of OPR's jurisdiction, or lacked supporting evidence. In such cases, we closed the matter without notifying the complainant.

When it is determined that an allegation requires further investigation, we initiate an inquiry by requesting additional details from the complainant, the subject, and/or relevant sources. If the provided information is sufficient to resolve the issue, we then conclude the inquiry.

When dealing with cases that cannot be easily resolved through written records or involve more serious concerns, we initiate a formal investigation. This process consists of gathering all relevant documents, speaking with witnesses, and conducting interviews with the individual involved. We only make findings of professional misconduct after completing a careful and thorough investigation.

We collaborated with internal and external partners, as well as various programs and offices, to ensure that allegations of employee misconduct were addressed appropriately. We also reviewed all critical incidents within the Department of Homeland Security (DHS). These investigations documented all events that transpired during essential incidents and, when necessary, presented them to the ICE Firearms and Use of Force Incident Review Committee for any action.

What is an allegation?

An allegation of misconduct is a report, either written or spoken, that suggests a federal employee may have acted unprofessionally, broken the law, or shown incompetence. It can also involve failing to adhere to standards of ethics, performance, or professional skills. People both outside and inside the organization can make these allegations. If the evidence indicates that misconduct occurred, the allegation is considered substantiated.

On the other hand, if there's not enough evidence, or if the evidence suggests the event didn't happen, the allegation is deemed unfounded.

We also investigated individuals within the United States and abroad who held Top Secret (TS) and Sensitive Compartmented Information (SCI) security clearances. My responsibilities included reviewing TS/SCI classified information, ensuring I could properly assess material that witnesses and investigation targets might also have access to.

Working in the SIU involved extensive travel. We investigated allegations from ICE offices in the United States, Canada, and Mexico, as well as cases from American embassies worldwide. The cases assigned varied, but each one was interesting.

On some occasions, government employees would become upset with their immediate supervisor or upper management and lodge an allegation accusing them of wrongdoing. Most of the time, it was just a case involving a disgruntled employee. There were times when, despite all that was said and done, upper management made mistakes, and I would have to document this in a report of investigation and present it for possible disciplinary action.

We investigated many cases, including shooting incidents involving DHS personnel. On multiple occasions, I personally reviewed cases where agents were involved in shootings, and in every investigation I conducted, these incidents were found to be justified.

OPR investigated allegations of misconduct at all levels of DHS, and investigations involved complex legal and ethical issues involving criminal prosecutions, national security matters, civil litigation, and other areas of the law overseen by DHS.

I was assigned a government vehicle to perform my investigative duties. Additionally, with the SIU office located in Alexandria, VA., I didn't have to relocate from my apartment at Braddock Apartments in Alexandria.

Working in OPR will show who your real friends are. Many people refer to working in internal affairs with phrases like 'entering the dark side.' This phrase is used to describe moving to OPR. Everyone recognized that OPR was essential for upholding ethical standards within our agency.

Working for OPR was challenging because recruiting agents was difficult, as they were aware that one day they would return to the field and have to work with individuals they may have previously investigated.

I had enough time in the agency, so I didn't have to worry about one day going back out in the field. I knew I could finish up my career in OPR and retire.

I learned that the agency hand-picks agents to work in OPR, and they chose me to conduct internal investigations. I was told that I was selected because I had a high level of integrity as an agent and I was loyal to the agency.

It's Not for Everybody

I will say that not everyone is suited to conduct investigations of allegations of employee misconduct. An OPR investigator must understand the sensitivity of an internal investigation and show respect to all employees in an attempt to foster mutual respect and cooperation.

Showing respect to employees was essential because I understood that the OPR function was meant to protect, not antagonize. During my investigations, I often met with department heads, ambassadors, and members of Congress.

For me, OPR was an assignment that I accepted with the understanding that I would be responsible for investigating fellow agents and employees with whom I had collaborated closely over many years.

OPR cases differed significantly from civilian investigations. The targeted employee I investigated had a similar level of knowledge of the law, investigative techniques, and interrogation tactics that I had. This made my job more difficult.

During many of my investigations, employees thought I was looking to find fault or assess blame; this was not my objective.

My objective was to be completely neutral, with no bias in either direction. I was trained that the allegations must be objectively investigated to a conclusion. I had to follow the evidence wherever it led me. On many occasions, my investigation cleared the employee of a serious crime or violation. However, I never know ahead of time what the case may uncover.

Conducting an OPR investigation requires maintaining professionalism and setting aside personal biases. Another aspect of a thorough OPR investigation was conducting all pertinent research. I carefully reviewed the incident report involving the employee, maintaining a thorough understanding of the agency's rules and regulations, and I was aware of the rights that the employee's job entails.

After working in OPR for a while, I realized that almost every employee will eventually become either a target or a witness in an OPR investigation at some point in their career.

Working in OPR served as a guardian of the agency's values, integrity, fairness, and service. By investigating misconduct, recommending corrective actions, and fostering a culture of accountability, Internal Affairs agents help ensure that ICE carries out its vital mission within the bounds of law and justice. Their work is both demanding and essential, forming a cornerstone of public trust in the agency and the broader framework of American law enforcement.

CHAPTER 17

Security Clearance

Starting my work with the U.S. Border Patrol, I was granted a security clearance of CONFIDENTIAL. This level of clearance enabled me to observe and review information that could reasonably be expected to cause harm to national security if disclosed without authorization.

When I transferred to the Immigration Inspections program and while working as an inspector, my security classification was upgraded to the SECRET level. This allowed me to review and observe information that the unauthorized disclosure could reasonably be expected to cause severe damage to national security.

I maintained a Secret clearance until I began work in the Examination Branch, where I was upgraded to the TOP SECRET level. This allowed me to review and observe information that could reasonably be expected to cause exceptionally grave damage to national security if disclosed unauthorized.

I maintained my Top Secret clearance until transferring to ICE Headquarters as the Section Chief. Working at this level required me to upgrade my security clearance to Top Secret.

Information above Top Secret means Sensitive Compartmented Information (SCI). It is not truly above Top Secret, since there is no clearance higher than Top Secret.

SCI information may be either Secret or Top Secret, but in either case, it has additional controls on dissemination beyond those associated with the classification level alone.

To gain SCI Access, I had to undergo a Single Scope Background Investigation (SSBI). Code words identify compartments of information. This is one means by which the "need to know" principle is formally and automatically enforced.

To access material within a specific SCI "compartment," an individual needs to have the appropriate clearance level for that material. The SCI designation itself is an additional layer, not a separate clearance level. For example, someone cleared at the SECRET level for a particular compartment X cannot view TOP SECRET information in that same compartment.

However, the opposite is true: a person with TOP SECRET clearance who has access to compartment X can also view SECRET material within it. Each compartment has a unique identifier, called a designator. These designators can also be classified or protected under another SCI compartment, adding an extra layer of security. A periodic reinvestigation is typically required every five years for Top Secret, depending on the agency. Access to a compartment of information is limited to the duration needed for a person to access a specific category of data. A Top Secret clearance with SCI (TS/SCI) is regarded as one of the highest levels of security clearance given to employees. To obtain my SCI eligibility, I had to be nominated for SCI access and approved by the agency.

Shortly after joining the Special Investigations Unit, I was required to maintain my security training to keep my TS/SCI clearance, which was necessary for performing my investigative duties.

As an investigator for the OPR SIU, I handled investigations involving individuals both in the United States and internationally who possess TS/SCI clearances. In this role, I was tasked with reviewing information classified at the TS/SCI level. To perform my duties effectively, I needed the ability to review material that witnesses and targets of investigations might also access.

TS/SCI clearance is the highest level of security clearance, granting agents access to the most highly classified and sensitive information. Issuing a TS/SCI full-scope clearance involves a comprehensive evaluation of an individual's trustworthiness, loyalty, and suitability for managing highly classified data. TS/SCI information must be managed through official access control systems established by the Director of National Intelligence. TS/SCI is not a classification level. At the same time, SCI clearance has been referred to as "Above Top Secret." Information at any classification level can be included within a TS/SCI control system.

Once declassified or decompartmentalized, this information is treated as collateral at the same classification level. The federal government mandates that TS/SCI materials be processed, stored, used, or discussed only within a Sensitive Compartmented Information Facility (SCIF). Within the context of the United States military, as well as in national security, national defense, and intelligence terminology, a SCIF (Sensitive Compartmented Information Facility) is defined as an enclosed space within a building designated for the processing of SCI (Sensitive Compartmented Information).

SCIFs may be either permanent or temporary and can be established within official government premises such as the Situation Room in the White House, aboard ships, within the private residences of officials, or in hotel rooms and other locations deemed necessary for officials during travel. Due to the operational security (OPSEC) risks they pose, personal cell phones, smart watches, computer flash drives, thumb drives, cameras (analog or digital) other than those owned by the U.S. Government and used only under strict guidelines, and any other recording or transmitting devices (analog or digital) are strictly prohibited in SCIFs.

CHAPTER 18

Certified Forensic Interviewer

Working at SIU was a wonderful experience, especially conducting assorted interviews and interrogations. In my position, I conducted investigations involving ICE directors, unit chiefs, program managers, and supervisors stationed in offices worldwide. When you initiate an investigation, it may involve numerous other employees or civilians who are also implicated in the allegation. It can also lead to separate independent investigations of civilians involved in crimes such as drugs, human smuggling, etc.

Government employees, especially criminal investigators (special agents), can find interview techniques challenging. Interviewing a criminal investigator as a witness, victim, or subject of an investigation can be a challenging experience. They do not like being interviewed or questioned, and it becomes a game you must play with them. All investigators believe they can outsmart you and walk away feeling like they've won the interview. While I was seeking the truth, most employees did everything possible to protect themselves or their co-workers, and they did not want to appear as if they were being "rats."

I had established sufficient training and work experience to

114

qualify myself as an expert witness in federal court on body language and deception detection. I conducted extensive interviews while teaching other investigators the concept of body language and micro-facial expressions.

As a leader in interview and interrogation training, management at OPR suggested that I continue my education by attending Forensic Interview and Interrogation training. I participated in a course on interview and interrogation, held in D.C., and completed an online study course within eight months. OPR covered the cost of the training, and after completing the course, I was required to take a written examination.

The course curriculum was through the International Association of Interviewers (IAI). I completed the twelve-month course in eight months and then scheduled my test. I was familiar with most of the material presented in the training, having received previous education, attended seminars, and completed numerous interview courses.

The material came extremely easily for me because I enjoyed it so much. I wanted to learn and know everything I could about conducting interviews and interrogations.

The Certified Forensic Interviewer is considered a professional with the expertise to conduct a variety of investigative interviews with victims, witnesses, suspects, or other sources to determine the facts regarding suspicions, allegations, or specific incidents in either public or private sector settings.

On January 24, 2010, I took the Certified Forensic Examiner test at the downtown D.C. library at 10:00 a.m. I completed the test in time with a few minutes to spare. The facility notified me after the test that I had passed the exam. A week later, I received my certificate of completion via mail, along with a certificate declaring me a Certified Forensic Interviewer on the national registry of forensic interviewers. This officially declared me an expert witness in federal courts for interview and interrogation techniques, body language, and micro-expressions.

After completing my certification, I assisted the Department of Homeland Security's training division with seminars on interview and interrogation techniques for ICE agents in field offices nationwide.

As a Certified Forensic Interviewer, I demonstrated an understanding of the legal aspects of interviewing and proficiency in interview preparation, behavioral analysis, accusatory and non-accusatory interviewing, documentation, and the presentation of findings.

I am unable to discuss many cases I was involved in, especially in this format. Some of these cases were extensive and involved criminal prosecutions. These cases demand and deserve privacy.

At this stage, I hold a TS/SCI security clearance and am a

certified forensic interviewer.

From the IAI/CFI website: The Certified Forensic Interview (CFI) program, developed by the International Association of Interviewers (IAI), aims to elevate the level of professionalism among all individuals and organizations involved in the field of interviewing.

The Certified Forensic Interviewer examination was developed by over 40 leading professionals, including experts in interviewing, law enforcement officials, and corporate representatives. Each member of the development team utilized their expertise to ensure the CFI examination addressed the core skill sets identified during extensive surveys of public and private sector interviewers and interrogators.

The objective of this certification program is to create comprehensive, universally accepted professional standards combined with an objective measure of an interviewer's knowledge of those standards. The ultimate goal is that every person and every organization with a stake in interviewing will benefit from the program, as will the reputation and effectiveness of the entire profession.

Art and Ethics

As agents, we often encounter individuals whose actions have caused significant harm or whose intentions could pose a threat to society's safety. These individuals are often called "very bad" because of their involvement in major crimes, terrorism, or organized crime, making their interrogation particularly challenging. The process isn't just about collecting information; it also involves navigating complex ethical questions, employing psychological techniques, and striking a balance between justice and compassion.

My team was dedicated to conducting thorough interrogations, and we all brought unique experiences to the table, from police detectives and federal investigators to experts in counterterrorism. Despite our different backgrounds, we united with a single goal in mind: to gather honest and practical intelligence that makes a real difference.

Agents were trained to interpret body language, identify deception, and use techniques that foster cooperation. Their work required a careful balance: being persistent without becoming coercive, effective while maintaining ethics, and determined without losing compassion.

Preparing agents for interrogation was a rigorous and multifaceted process. It involved not only learning interview techniques, but also understanding the psychology of those who commit grievous acts.

On many occasions, the agency invested in ongoing education, bringing in experts in behavioral science, linguistics, and cultural studies. Agents were taught to recognize when a subject was withholding information, to adapt their approach based on the individual's background, and to remain cognizant of legal boundaries.

Keep in mind that interrogating those who have committed serious offenses demands psychological sophistication. Agents must understand what motivates such individuals: some are driven by ideology, others by profit, while deeply rooted personal grievances drive others. By identifying the subject's motives, we could tailor our strategy to build rapport or gently challenge inconsistencies in their accounts.

We employed various strategies during the interrogation of high-risk subjects. There is no one-size-fits-all solution; agents must possess a toolbox of approaches, each suited to the different scenarios they face.

Our interview methods employed a structured approach: first, non-accusatory interviewing to establish baseline behavior, followed by a transition to accusatory questioning if deception was detected. The technique makes use of psychological manipulation, alternating between pressure and empathy, to elicit confessions or valuable information.

On occasion, we used cognitive interviewing, a more conversational method designed to help subjects access and recount their memories. We guided individuals through the process of reconstructing events in as much detail as possible, often asking them to recall the scenario from multiple perspectives or in reverse order. This technique was helpful when we were dealing with reluctant witnesses or those affected by some form of trauma.

We also had to build rapport. When you can establish a rapport, it is often the key to successful information gathering. When we showed respect, understanding, and patience, we could encourage even the most hardened individuals to open up.

Rapport-building may involve discussing neutral topics, expressing concern for the subject's well-being, or finding common ground. This approach stands in stark contrast to the stereotype of harsh, adversarial questioning.

Sometimes, confrontation with the individual was needed. We provided evidence, pointed out contradictions, or questioned doubtful statements. When questioning those suspected of serious misconduct, it was crucial to remain calm and composed, relying on facts and logic rather than emotion to steer the discussion.

The agent's ability to detect deception was crucial during interrogations. We were trained to observe micro-expressions, brief facial movements that can indicate concealed emotions, as well as shifts in speech, posture, and eye behavior. Although we occasionally used polygraphs or other technological tools, human intuition was always vital.

We also had to consider ethical implications. When interrogating individuals accused of serious crimes carries enormous moral weight. International law, including conventions such as the United Nations Convention Against Torture, strictly forbids the use of torture or inhumane treatment. We were tasked with obtaining information without crossing these boundaries.

But even when facing individuals responsible for grave acts, we had to adhere to principles of proportionality and justice. The desire to protect society couldn't justify the abandonment of humane treatment. Effective interrogation was best accomplished through psychological tactics rather than physical coercion. Respect for the rights and dignity of all persons remained important.

We also had to deal with the legal framework. We operated within strict legal constraints. Any information obtained illegally or through coercive means was inadmissible in court. We had to remain aware of relevant laws regarding detention, questioning, and the right to counsel. Detailed documentation of all interactions was standard practice, ensuring accountability and transparency.

The interrogation of dangerous individuals was burdened with challenges. Some subjects may be highly trained in resisting questions, using silence, misdirection, or outright lies as shields.

Others may be psychologically unstable, making it difficult to distinguish truth from delusion. We were vigilant for manipulation and remained steadfast in our pursuit of accuracy.

Some agents experienced emotional strain from repeatedly encountering individuals who committed heinous acts, which could have psychological repercussions. We became more aware of our mental health needs, yet support options like counseling, peer support, and resilience training were often our only resources. The danger of vicarious trauma, where an agent is affected by the suffering or cruelty of others, was widely recognized.

In some interviews, we encountered subjects who were brilliant, ideologically committed, and uncooperative. We started by establishing rapport and exploring their personal history and motivations. As the conversation progressed, inconsistencies in earlier statements emerged. By tailoring our questions to fit their worldview, we gently prompted the individual to disclose information that could help prevent future crimes.

In another case, we interviewed a leader of a criminal syndicate. The subject attempted to intimidate and manipulate the interview. We responded with calm persistence, methodically presenting evidence and drawing out details. By remaining unshaken and showing a little respect, we eventually secured a confession that brought closure to several unsolved cases.

Human trafficking cases were especially complex, given the trauma experienced by victims and the cunning of perpetrators. We approached these interrogations delicately, striking a balance between the need for justice and the desire for empathy. By focusing on fact-finding and offering security to those affected, we had dismantled trafficking rings and secured vital intelligence for future operations.

Interrogating individuals with a history of misconduct was an endeavor that demanded intellect, empathy, and unwavering ethical standards. Agents had to strike a balance between the urgent demands of justice and a profound respect for human dignity. The challenge was an ongoing one, as new threats and new techniques arose.

Interviewing and interrogating are not merely technical skills; they are arts, grounded in psychology, ethics, and human connection. A successful outcome depended on preparation, empathy, and unwavering integrity.

The main goal wasn't just about gathering information; it was also about doing so in a way that showed respect for the person and upheld the truth. The skills of interviewing and the science of interrogation are invaluable tools, mainly when used responsibly and thoughtfully.

Conversational Hypnosis

Conversational hypnosis, also known as covert hypnosis, is a gentle and approachable method of communication that utilizes subtle language, rapport-building techniques, and gentle suggestions to help others become more relaxed and receptive. While it's often used in therapy or negotiation settings, the friendly principles behind conversational hypnosis can also positively influence how interviews are conducted.

By integrating hypnotic techniques into questioning and dialogue, interviewers can create a warm and trusting environment that fosters honesty, openness, and genuine connection, leading to deeper and more meaningful conversations.

Conversational hypnosis was built on hypnotherapy, which emphasizes indirect suggestion, storytelling, metaphors, and the natural rhythms of conversation. Unlike traditional hypnosis, it does not require formal trance induction or the subject's explicit awareness of hypnotic intent. Instead, it relies on building rapport, creating a sense of safety and trust, so the individual feels at ease.

Using specific phrases and structures that bypass resistance and encourage subconscious agreement. Mirroring the individual's reality before gently guiding them toward new perspectives or responses. Engaging the imagination and emotion can soften defenses and foster openness.

Before delving into techniques, it is essential to stress the ethical context. Conversational hypnosis in interviews must be used with respect for autonomy, confidentiality, and consent. The goal was not manipulation, but to foster a space where authentic communication could flourish. We avoided using these skills to coerce, deceive, or elicit information from someone against their will.

Interviewing with conversational hypnosis was not about wielding secret power, but about cultivating a respectful, attentive, and gently influential environment. By using rapport, attentive listening, and hypnotic language patterns, interviewers could facilitate conversations that are more authentic, revealing, and meaningful.

When used ethically, these skills enhance the interview process and emphasize the unique stories and perspectives of those we encounter.

CHAPTER 19

OPR Houston, Texas

While at SIU, I was asked if I wanted to get closer to home in Louisiana. Of course, I said yes, and the proposal was that OPR wanted to open an office in Houston for the Management Inspections Unit (MIU). My job offer was to move to Houston and establish a new MIU office. I accepted the position and arranged to relocate to Houston.

On May 28th, I started working as a Senior Special Agent in the OPR MIU. I met with the Resident Agent in Charge (RAC) for OPR investigations, who showed me around the office, including the three designated offices where I would establish the new MIU offices.

My assignment was to set up the new MIU office in Houston, preparing the office for three other agents to arrive. I was tasked with setting up the office, receiving furniture, and organizing many office supplies that were to come.

A few days after I arrived, two additional special agents assigned to MIU arrived to help me set up the new office. OPR headquarters had previously sent several boxes of office supplies, file cabinets, desks, and various government forms for MIU use. Eventually, our main computers and programs arrived, and we started setting up our new MIU office.

After several weeks of sorting, arranging, and organizing the office, we were ready to assume our official duties. By this point, HQ started sending us our work assignments. We were officially operational as an MIU office.

MIU Duties

One of our functions was to inspect ICE directorates, programs, and field offices to verify and ensure compliance with established federal, departmental, agency, or program-specific policies and procedures.

Our MIU inspections would highlight to ICE leadership any areas that need attention, resources, or improvement in the office that we inspected.

When we conducted an MIU inspection, we included financial audits of the agency's Certified Undercover Operations to ensure that the undercover financial activities were adequately accounted for in accordance with law and agency policy.

We conducted inspections of each 287(g) program to ensure its effectiveness and compliance with the agency's requirements. The 287(g) program enabled state and local law enforcement agencies to partner with ICE to identify and remove incarcerated criminal non-citizens who were amenable to deportation from the United States before they were released into the community. Through this program, state and local law enforcement agencies collaborate with the federal government to enforce federal immigration laws.

We also assisted agency field offices and headquarters programs with assessing their compliance with agency policies and procedures.

We performed on-site inspections of domestic and international ICE field offices and ICE Headquarters Units. The process included a thorough review of operational and administrative procedures to provide ICE senior managers with an independent evaluation of the office's internal controls, effectiveness, and efficiency.

During my brief tenure at MIU, from May 28, 2010, to February 1, 2011, I made numerous trips around the country to perform inspections of ICE field offices. Those offices included Atlanta, Boston, Buffalo, Chicago, Cleveland, Denver, El Paso, Guam, Hawaii, Las Vegas, Long Beach, Nogales, New York, Burlington, San Antonio, Seattle, Tampa, Miami, and many more cities across the United States and U.S. territories.

The inspection process typically took three to five days at each office, and my duty was to interview employees working in those offices to determine their knowledge of policies and procedures. These interviews were conducted more as informal talks than formal interviews, allowing me to determine if the office required additional training or resources.

On February 2, 2011, I received a phone call late that afternoon from the ICE OPR Deputy Director, who asked if I wanted to return to investigations and work at the OPR New Orleans field office. I told him I could be there that night and ready to go the next day, but he laughed at me and told me to clear out my case reports for the MIU inspections we were conducting, and he would be back in touch with me soon.

I enjoyed working in Houston, specifically at MIU. I would have been comfortable working in the Houston office if the New Orleans position hadn't come. I couldn't pass up the opportunity to return to Amite and live in my home again.

The New Orleans OPR would allow me to conduct investigations again, which is where I wanted to be.

I received my official transfer orders to OPR New Orleans several days later.

CHAPTER 20

OPR New Orleans, Louisiana

As I mentioned, I was thrilled when the OPR Assistant Director called me in Houston to discuss transferring to New Orleans. I expected the transfer to take months to come through, but I received it within weeks.

The OPR New Orleans (OPR NO) Investigations office was located in the Entergy Building downtown. My office had a great view of the Superdome and downtown, allowing me to see Mardi Gras parades and immigration protests below.

OPR Duties

The OPR NO cases I was assigned were similar to those I investigated with the SIU. However, I had a five-state area of responsibility in New Orleans, investigating allegations related to all DHS/ICE employees and other criminal accusations. These states included Louisiana, Mississippi, Arkansas, Tennessee, and Alabama, encompassing thirty-five ICE offices. This was considered our Area of Responsibility (AOR).

Additionally, there were numerous ICE detention facilities within these states, housing several thousand detainees awaiting deportation or immigration hearings.

At OPR NO, we collaborated with internal and external programs and offices to guarantee that allegations of misconduct against employees were handled appropriately and equitably, while also ensuring that the process was conducted swiftly. Additionally, we conducted reviews of all critical incidents, including employee-involved shootings, that occurred within ICE offices in our jurisdiction.

Our investigations documented the events that transpired during critical incidents, and when necessary, they were presented to the ICE Firearms and Use of Force Incident Review Committee for review and action.

We examined issues that could result in criminal prosecution or significant administrative misconduct, which an ICE manager would handle.

The OPR NO office comprises three special agents, a supervisory special agent, and an investigative assistant. Although the OPR NO was small in personnel, it covered all assigned ICE offices within the five-state area.

Before my report day, Linda and I visited my new office to familiarize ourselves with the environment and meet the other agents. All of my shipped belongings were waiting for me inside the office when I arrived. My office was huge and way more room than I needed. It was close to 300 feet of workspace. One side of my wall was entirely made of glass, from the ceiling to the floor.

Of course, Linda ended up decorating my office and putting everything in its rightful place. That meant taking down things I had already hung and moving them to other locations. She rehung everything on the walls and rearranged the furniture after I had placed it where I "thought" I wanted it. But when she was done, I had to admit that it did look great!

With Linda being my interior designer, the other agents in the office were jealous because their offices didn't look as professional as mine. The other agents would come around in the afternoons and stop by my door to stare into my office, admiring what Linda had done. I know they picked up a few ideas because their offices made some changes for the better.

My only problem was keeping the dust down and keeping everything clean. The cleaning lady for our offices kept my office pretty clean because she knew Linda had been there. At times, I gave her a few extra dollars to keep my office especially clean for me, especially when Linda was coming to visit.

OPR NO also managed the Prison Rape Elimination Act (PREA) program within our AOR, coordinating with other OPR offices and other investigative entities to address sexual assault allegations involving ICE detainees.

The Prison Rape Elimination Act was passed in 2003 to

combat and prevent sexual violence in correctional facilities throughout the United States. Its main aim is to eliminate prisoner sex offenses in all types of correctional institutions, including prisons, jails, and juvenile detention centers.

I was assigned cases where detainees being held in detention facilities within our AOR reported allegations, such as that another detainee had raped them. The majority of these cases involved detainees. But, I have investigated numerous instances in which the detention officer had a relationship with a detainee and either got caught by staff members or other detainees reported it to the facility. The detention facility officers were contract workers hired by several different companies.

Now, what is the difference between an inmate and a detainee? An inmate refers to a person who is confined to a prison or correctional facility serving out a term. An ICE detainee is an individual who is held in custody by ICE due to immigration-related issues. This can occur when someone is placed on an immigration hold or detainer, which allows ICE to take custody of the individual for immigration proceedings after they have been detained by local law enforcement for other reasons.

ICE detainees were normally held in detention facilities waiting for an immigration hearing or waiting to be deported from the United States.

Giglio/Henthorn program. This program responds to impeachment requests from the U.S. Department of Justice concerning ICE employees who may serve as government witnesses or affiants in federal criminal proceedings.

Ethical Investigation

Let's clear up a common source of confusion: an ethical investigation isn't the same as an ethics investigation. An ethics investigation examines whether an individual's actions have violated ethical guidelines—think of it as the 'why' behind workplace misconduct. On the other hand, an ethical investigation is about ensuring that the entire investigative process is handled with integrity, fairness, and transparency. The primary purpose of an ethical inquiry is to provide a fair evaluation of what happened, why it happened, and how employers can prevent it in the future. This process typically begins with thoroughly examining the case's aspects, including identifying the wrong, who was involved, and why it happened.

At its core, an ethical investigation ensures that every step, from gathering facts to making decisions, is unbiased, consistent, and respectful of everyone involved. It's not just about reaching the right conclusion—it's about how you get there. That means protecting confidentiality, following clear protocols, and treating employees with dignity. When investigations are handled ethically, employees are more likely to trust the process, speak up when issues arise, and believe in their organization's commitment to fairness.

CHAPTER 21

Sex Scandal

I am unable to discuss each case I investigated while assigned to OPR NO; however, I wish to highlight a particular case that I found especially intriguing. I estimate that I conducted over 500 investigations during my tenure at the New Orleans OPR.

Prostitution Sex Scandal Case

In 2013, I conducted an investigation concerning allegations that ICE Enforcement and Removal Operations (ERO) Detention Officers (DOs) engaged in sexual conduct with minor prostitutes during deportation journeys to Thailand, Malaysia, Vietnam, and the Philippines. A recently recruited DO reported these allegations to the Office of Professional Responsibility (OPR NO).

This DO (complainant) said that when he was assigned to escort individuals back to Thailand or other countries, his fellow DOs traveling with him would participate in prostitution while visiting the sex strip clubs. He alleged that after turning the escorted detainees over to the representative of that country, they would have at least a two-day turnaround before they were able to travel back to the U.S. Still, during the waiting period, the other DOs would visit sex clubs and bring young females back to their hotel rooms.

The complainant said he believed that some of them were underage females. The complainant stated that he filed the allegation because he didn't wish to participate in or work with the DOs in such an environment, fearing he would be implicated in a scandal.

I was assigned to investigate the allegation and gather all necessary facts for either a criminal case or an administrative review, as needed.

One of the responsibilities of an ICE Deportation Officer (DO) is to facilitate the transportation of noncitizens who have been judicially ordered for deportation by a federal court to their country of origin. This authority is conferred under the Immigration and Nationality Act.

ICE removes noncitizens from the United States after they have received a final order of removal. These removal operations require complex coordination, management, and facilitation efforts to remove and return noncitizens to their respective countries successfully. ERO DOs accomplished this mission through charter flights, commercial airlines for escorted and unescorted removals, and ground transportation missions on the northern and southern borders and at ports of entry.

ERO handles removals of fugitives wanted for serious crimes abroad, including homicide, gang offenses, corruption, fraud, and terrorism. This includes individuals on the terrorist watch list and no-fly list, as well as war criminals and human rights abusers such as those involved in torture, ethnic cleansing, and genocide. High-profile removals are escorted out of the U.S. via commercial flights, ICE charters, or military charters, often handed over to law enforcement in their home countries.

I interviewed the complainant for two hours, and he described what he had witnessed during his foreign travel with DOs from around the United States. He explained in detail what the DOs did when they arrived in various countries.

The complaint explained that on multiple occasions, flights from New Orleans would arrive in a particular country while flights from other ICE locations would also arrive there simultaneously. When that happened, all the DOs knew one another, and they would all stay in the same hotel. The complainant provided the names of the DOs from the assorted offices.

After interviewing the complainant, I covertly requested through the OPR HQ all the travel logs from the DOs' offices, which showed the names of the DOs assigned to travel, along with the dates and locations, over the past six months. By ordering the records this way, no one from the DO's office would know I ordered them.

Upon receiving the information, I could review who the DOs were who traveled during those dates and who traveled as a team. This allowed me to verify some of the complainant's information.

Over the next seven months, I interviewed twenty-three DOs from various offices as subjects of the investigation and twenty-one other employees as witnesses. The result of these interviews was that I opened twenty-two investigative cases on DOs.

After each DO was interviewed, all but one admitted to some form of criminal misconduct while they were on official travel status overseas. Luckily, not one admitted to having any encounters with underage females.

Most DOs admitted to attempting to have sex but didn't, and some admitted they wanted to have sex but did not have the money. One DO explained he never tried to have sex or make any contact with any females while traveling overseas. I closed his case and listed it as unfounded.

I listed the other twenty-two investigative cases as substantiated cases. I forwarded them to the Director of OPR, who would forward the findings to the Director of Detention and Deportation for any disciplinary action regarding the DOs.

Keep in mind that I didn't have enough physical evidence of

any criminal wrongdoing other than a statement from the complainant, who admitted that he never knew if the other DOs had ever had sex with any of the foreign nationals.

During my interviews, I approached the situation cautiously, extracting information while maintaining the appearance of being fully aware of their activities. Due to the lack of concrete evidence to support a criminal conviction in federal court, I was only able to obtain an admission of misconduct. Consequently, I handled these cases as administrative rather than criminal investigations.

Our federal law provides "extraterritorial jurisdiction" over certain sex offenses against underage children. Extraterritorial jurisdiction is the legal authority of the United States to prosecute criminal conduct outside its borders. You have to realize that Federal Statute prohibits United States citizens or legal permanent residents from traveling from the United States to a foreign country and, while there, raping or sexually molesting a child or paying a child for sex.

Citizens can be punished under this law even if their conduct was legal in the country where it occurred. For example, if an individual traveled to a country that had legalized prostitution, and while they were there, they paid an underage girl for sex, that individual could still be convicted under this statute in the United States. The penalty for this provision is up to 30 years in prison.

Also, under a similar provision, it is a crime for United States citizens or legal permanent residents to travel from the United States to a foreign country with the intent to engage in illegal sexual conduct with a child, such as rape, molestation, or prostitution. The agency administratively held the final results of these cases in a sealed status, pending punishment.

Subsequently, based on the investigation's findings, procedures concerning the international travel of DOs and the activities permitted during their travel were revised.

Just a note, to make a good criminal case, I would have had to travel to that country, locate the female in question, and interview her. That would be hunting a needle in a haystack.

CHAPTER 22

Assistant Director's Award

On April 2, 2014, I was presented with the Assistant Director's "2013 Excellence in Investigation Award" from the U.S. Department of Homeland Security, Homeland Security Investigations.

The award presentation took place at the Department of Homeland Security office in New Orleans. Presenting the award were Assistant Director Tim Moynihan and Special Agent in Charge David D'Amato, both from Washington, D.C.

The Assistant Director's Award is an opportunity to recognize the significant contributions of an employee who has advanced the mission of the Department of Homeland Security, Homeland Security Investigations, during the year.

During the presentation, Assistant Director Moynihan said, "Special Agent Smith has performed above and beyond the call of duty. He has conducted significant and diverse high-profile investigations that he has pursued thoroughly, tirelessly, and professionally. He is a determined agent with tremendous interview skills; he encompasses all the qualities of what a Special Agent should be."

"Donnie is also a Certified Forensic Interviewer for the Department of Homeland Security and travels all over the United States conducting interviews pertaining to suspected criminal activity."

One of the reasons I received the award was that I investigated several significant cases within one year.

The most prominent case I handled involved twenty defendants involved in prostitution and child pornography, both domestically and internationally. The seven-month investigation included over 25 witness interviews and 20 targeted interviews.

Eighteen cases were substantiated, while two remain unsubstantiated due to insufficient evidence to secure convictions. Due to the secrecy of the case, I collaborated with one other agent and wrote every investigation report and closing report for each case.

CHAPTER 23

You Never Know Who's Watching

Here's a brief overview of one case I investigated, which is representative of many similar instances where illegal immigrants persuaded government employees into doing things they usually wouldn't do. I'm excluding specific details such as names and location, and focusing on the core aspects.

In March 2014, an ICE agent was residing in a city in Arkansas, married with three children, living in a small subdivision. He and his wife had been experiencing ongoing conflicts within their marriage. They argued frequently, partly because he was working long hours during the week.

The agent was at a local service station one morning getting gas when he noticed a woman with two children also getting gas. He spoke to her, and a conversation started. Over the next few weeks, he saw the woman and her children at the gas station, and each time they talked. He eventually asked her to dinner, and she agreed. They went out several times, which helped them get to know each other better.

During an evening outing, he asked her about her past relationships and her limited English skills. She explained that she was from Ecuador and that she and her husband had been separated for a few months. She told the agent that she and her boyfriend had entered the United States illegally two years ago with their two children. They crossed the Mexican border in South Texas, where they met family members and stayed until they moved to the same city as the agent. Keep in mind that during her story, she was unaware of the agent's professional role.

After she finished her story, he explained what he did for a living, but assured her that she was not in danger of being arrested and had nothing to worry about.

In summary, their relationship developed closer. They started seeing each other more often, with him helping to pay her bills and buy clothes for her children. Of course, the agent's wife remained unaware of this arrangement.

The agent's next-door neighbor owned a business with several hundred employees in town. They were friends and often saw each other on Saturdays while mowing the lawn. The neighbor was aware of the problems the agent and his wife faced. Knowing where the agent worked, the neighbor had asked for help on multiple occasions to speed up the hiring process at his business.

The people the neighbor wanted to hire were from various countries, not U.S. citizens. He asked the agent to run criminal background checks on their names to expedite the hiring process for him. The neighbor needed to submit the names to the immigration processing center for approval before hiring. He wanted the agent to accelerate the hiring process as a favor. The agent refused, explaining that, as an agent, he was not authorized to provide such services to private businesses. The neighbor stated he understood and dropped the request, for now.

Over several months, the agent and his wife had a severe argument. She packed her belongings with the children and moved to her mother's house in Northern Arkansas. For several days, the agent mostly went to work and returned home in the evenings. When he was not at home, he stayed at his Ecuadorian girlfriend's house, which was in a nearby trailer park outside of town.

The agent's wife had been absent for weeks and was not expected to return in the near future. The agent extended an invitation to the girlfriend to stay with him; however, she was required to arrive after sunset to prevent others from seeing her and the children entering the residence.

The agent departed for work promptly at 5:00 a.m. each morning, necessitating her to awaken early and leave with him. This routine persisted for several days, during which all matters proceeded smoothly.

One night, the neighbor couldn't sleep and was walking around his house, heading toward the kitchen. Around 11:00

p.m., he looked out the kitchen window toward the agent's house and saw the agent with his girlfriend in their kitchen, hugging. The neighbor recognized that it wasn't his wife.

At 5:00 a.m., the neighbor looked out the front window again and saw the girlfriend and the agent leaving in separate cars. Over the next few days, he observed the girlfriend coming and going under the cover of darkness.

One Saturday afternoon, the neighbor, while cutting his grass, observed the agent walking around in his yard. He approached and initiated a conversation. The neighbor informed the agent that he had seen the girlfriend walking inside the house and had also observed the children moving about in the yard at night. The agent was astonished, believing he was discreetly seeing his girlfriend without anyone's knowledge. He explained to the neighbor that he and his wife were temporarily separated while they attempted to resolve some issues.

The neighbor assured the agent that he had no concerns, as he would not disclose this information to anyone. The agent appreciated the reassurance, as he preferred that his wife remain unaware of the situation.

A few days later, the neighbor returned to discuss with the agent the possibility of running criminal checks on potential employees. He mentioned that he had been keeping quiet about his girlfriend as a favor, but now he's asking for one in return.

He handed the agent a list of names and requested record checks, followed by approval to proceed with hiring the individuals listed.

The agent believed that if he didn't run the names, the neighbor might betray him to his wife out of spite. Despite knowing this was against policy and risking his job, he still took the names and later shared the information with the neighbor.

About a week later, the neighbor gave the agent another list of names. The agent refused, but the neighbor reminded him that he had information about his wife, and the agent had also done something he shouldn't have. Realizing his predicament, the agent saw no choice but to continue assisting the neighbor with his request.

Eventually, the agent and his wife filed for divorce, and he moved his girlfriend and her children into his house. After that, the neighbor stopped asking him to run criminal background checks on employees.

It wasn't long before the girlfriend confronted the agent, who had been employed at a local fast-food place and was earning an income. She informed the agent that she held a reputable position there and had been employed for approximately one year. The agent asked her how she managed to secure employment despite being in the country illegally. She candidly disclosed to him that upon her arrival in the U.S., she had arranged to purchase fraudulent documents from an individual in the vicinity. She subsequently used those documents to secure employment, enabling her to care for her children.

The agent was upset, but he understood that something was happening that required her to take care of the children. Later, he said he believed the ex-boyfriend was sending her money for that purpose. She pleaded with the agent not to disclose this and to let her keep working at the restaurant. He chose to remain silent, and in doing so, he committed multiple crimes.

The neighbor made several more requests to the agent to check a list of names, but the agent refused, citing that he and his wife were getting a divorce and his secrets no longer mattered.

The neighbor, knowing the girlfriend was illegal, reported everything to the Department of Homeland Security's internal affairs division, Office of Professional Responsibility (OPR). He shared the entire story about the agent, including several lists of names the agent had checked and returned for his business.

I was assigned to investigate the matter to determine its accuracy. I began by compiling computer records related to the names the agent searched for the neighbor. This system allowed me to see the agent's login name and who initiated the search. It also showed the time and date when the search was conducted.

I conducted a detailed interview with the neighbor at a private location. After collecting his statement, I conducted surveillance on the agent's residence. I monitored the property and identified the vehicle driven by the girlfriend, including its license plate. I also captured clear photos of her and the children arriving and leaving the home. Using this information, I obtained copies of her driver's license. I surveilled the residence for over a week, observing that the girlfriend and her children were essentially living there with the agent.

I conducted a thorough immigration check on the girlfriend, the name listed on the vehicle registration, the driver's license, and other documents that I was able to obtain. The results showed that the papers the girlfriend was using belonged to a deceased woman who had passed away a year before the girlfriend arrived in the United States. The date of birth was similar to the girlfriend's, so the ages would align if anyone verified. The name on the fraud document was that of a Hispanic woman who lived and died in Arizona. Therefore, the name also matched the girlfriend's Ecuadorian background.

I then went to the restaurant where the girlfriend said she worked and conducted surveillance to document her coming and going from the restaurant.

One day, I watched her leave the restaurant around 3:00 p.m. When she left the restaurant, I approached the manager to inquire about the girlfriend's hiring status. The manager provided me with the necessary employment documents, and I discovered that she had applied for work as a U.S. citizen using false documents.

Several days later, I was watching the agent's house when he came out with the two children. He placed them in his government work vehicle and started driving away. I managed to follow him and tracked him to a school where he dropped off the children. Afterward, he left the school and headed to his office. That is another violation; using a government vehicle to transport passengers for personal reasons is prohibited. It's considered misuse of a government vehicle and could result in disciplinary action, including termination of employment.

A few days later, I identified the route the girlfriend took each day to reach work at the restaurant. I wanted to interview the girlfriend, so I contacted the local police department and requested that they make a traffic stop so I could speak with her. I had enough information to arrest her, but I wanted to talk with her first and see what she was willing to tell me. I had previously spoken with the U.S. Attorney, and she was aware of my progress.

The local police conducted a traffic stop on the girlfriend's vehicle, and I approached to speak with her. I had a conference room reserved at my hotel for interviews. I escorted her there and advised her to be honest and tell the truth.

From the beginning, she claimed to be a U.S. citizen,

contradicting the information I had. Her ability to speak English was decent, but I had an agent there who spoke fluent Spanish to ensure clear communication.

It took some time talking with her, but she eventually admitted everything regarding the fraudulent documents, her relationship with the agent, and her job at the restaurant. During her statement, she explained that she used the agent to get what she needed: security. She said that when she first met the agent, she recognized him and had seen him before. I never fully believed that part, but her details about the documents were accurate. She even gave me the name of the person from whom she purchased the documents.

She became angry, saying the person who sold her the documents claimed they were foolproof. So, that is why she decided to expose everyone. She also told me about the list of names that the agent had run for the neighbor. The more she talked, the angrier she got. She was mad, feeling that if she were going down, everyone around her would follow suit. By then, she knew she was under arrest, and she wanted to take everyone down with her.

After taking care of her arrest processing and preparing her jail booking information, I turned her over to the U.S. Marshals for further processing. I returned to the restaurant and informed the manager of what had transpired. I told him that she had admitted to everything, and I even mentioned that she was providing information about everyone involved in her scheme.

At that point, the restaurant manager just stared at me, and I asked him several times what the problem was. He said he needed to speak with someone about the entire issue. I took him to the hotel conference room, and we had a long conversation while I took his statement. The manager explained that he knew she was not legal and that the documents were counterfeit. He explained that her boyfriend, the agent, and another man came by one afternoon and asked him to keep her as an employee because they were using her as an informant, and she needed work. So, that is why he allowed her to work there. He thought he was helping out the government.

I showed the manager a photo lineup that included the agent's photo and five other people matching the same description, and he identified the agent from the lineup.

By now, you understand the situation. The agent was arrested and later served time in jail for his actions. The girlfriend also served time in prison before being deported, and her children went to stay with her sister, who was a permanent resident living in the United States. The restaurant manager was not arrested.

It goes to show, you never know who's watching.

The issue of harboring illegal aliens is a complex and sensitive one, involving layers of legal, ethical, and social considerations.

153

This term generally refers to the act of knowingly providing shelter, aid, or assistance to individuals who are present in a country in violation of immigration laws.

CHAPTER 24

Jail Guard Arrested

In the following case, I have omitted details such as names and locations.

In July 2015, I was assigned a case involving multiple thefts at a county jail in Alabama. Numerous allegations were made by ICE detainees stating that while they were booked in and housed there, they relinquished their belongings, including money, credit cards, jewelry, and other personal items, to the jail. This county jail was contracted by ICE to house detainees for short periods.

When the detainees were transported out of the facility to another location, their belongings were not returned to them. Detainees complained that their credit cards were missing, and the facility said they couldn't be found. The detainees stated that the facility had promised them that if they found the missing items, they would forward them to their next facility; however, all the detainees reported that this had never happened.

When I started investigating the case, I found it odd that detainees being transferred out of the facility were missing their credit cards. Numerous allegations implied either widespread carelessness or theft by the facility staff. Money, I can see someone stealing, but credit cards?

I went to the facility and spoke with a detective from the sheriff's office. After reviewing several months of records, I requested employee schedules and booking sheets from the jail. It became clear that the same deputy booked detainees who reported missing credit cards. The deputy was involved in inventorying detainees' property, placing it in labeled clear plastic bags, and storing it in the jail safe. Upon release or transfer, the property was returned to the detainees after they had signed for it. In 20 cases of missing credit cards, the same deputy had processed each of the detainees.

After identifying this deputy, I reviewed the surveillance videos from the days and nights he worked, watching him process the detainees during his shift. While working closely with the Sheriff's Office investigator one evening, we both watched as this deputy booked detainees into the facility. Still, we did not see anything out of the ordinary.

I arranged with our ICE detention office in the area to borrow a detainee who was a trustee at another facility to assist me with my investigation. The investigator for the Sheriff's Office pretended to have arrested this trustee and brought him to the jail for processing on the day the suspected deputy was working. We placed several credit cards we obtained from a previous case and gave the name on the card to the trustee. The trustee was from Morocco, and we instructed him not to speak English, although he was fluent in the language.

The Sheriff's investigator brought the trustee in through the usual process to the jail and turned it over to the suspected deputy for processing. We knew how much money and credit cards were on the trustee, so we sat back and waited.

When the suspect deputy's shift ended, the investigator and I went to review the processing paperwork and check if the credit cards were in the plastic evidence bag in the safe. When we checked the evidence bag, we found that the credit cards were inside as required. It didn't appear that anything was missing from the trustee's property. We checked the other bags as well, and the short version is that nothing was missing from any of the property bags. Did the suspected deputy go straight, or is he waiting for another time?

The Sheriff's investigator and I were very confused as we determined where to go next. We watched for several days, and nothing happened. Without any objective evidence or proof, we had no basis for making an arrest.

After discussing with the investigator, we have agreed to start interviews with all relevant individuals to gather information. If these interviews do not produce significant findings, I will temporarily close the cases until more information becomes available.

We began scheduling interviews with all the deputies who

worked in the facility. After conducting numerous interviews, I began to receive information about two deputies who didn't get along well and were consistently disgruntled.

Additionally, I found out that a supervisory role at the jail will soon be announced. The two deputies I interviewed were competing for this position. One of the deputies was our primary suspect, now identified as Deputy #1, while the other is known as Deputy #2. Both of them worked together on different shifts at the processing center.

After reviewing the shifts when Deputy #2 worked, I discovered that Deputy #2 worked with Deputy #1 only a couple of times a week. I then focused my interviews on these two individuals, pressing them extremely hard. Deputy #2 admitted to not caring for Deputy #1 much, and he frequently discussed detainees missing credit cards and other items when they were released or transferred.

It occurred to me while interviewing him that he knew a great deal about the case and was making numerous accusations against Deputy #1. I asked Deputy #2 numerous questions that he would have had no way of knowing, but he knew the answers to them. Throughout our interview, Deputy #2 mentioned Deputy #1 on three occasions, repeatedly discussing how he consistently makes mistakes in his job.

Whenever I interviewed Deputy #1, he showed remorse and

discussed how sad it was for the detainees not to have their property returned. He spoke about his procedures and could not understand where things went wrong. Remember that after one of his shifts, we reviewed his work and found that our detainees' items were processed correctly and placed in the safe with no mistakes.

After completing all my interviews, I began to think very hard about Deputy #2. On the fourth interview with Deputy # 2, I went for it. I told him I knew everything and that he was returning to the safe to retrieve items after the deputies had processed them and put them away. It took some time, but Deputy #2 eventually admitted that he did not like Deputy #1 and was aware that he was competing with him for the supervisor position. Deputy #2 admitted that he would sometimes go to the safe and remove credit cards from detainees' bags that Deputy #1 had previously processed. He said that he did this in the hope that Deputy #1 would be fired, leaving him as the only candidate deserving of the vacant supervisor position.

On August 5, 2015, Deputy #2 was arrested during a joint investigation by the Department of Homeland Security, OPR New Orleans, and the County Sheriff's Office. Deputy #2 faced charges of tampering with government records and pleaded guilty to a felony, receiving a sentence of two years' probation and a $1,500 fine. He was terminated on the day of his arrest.

159

For my efforts, the county Sheriff presented me with a special pocket knife featuring the Sheriff's logo. In reality, this was an item he handed out to all visitors from other agencies.

CHAPTER 25

Reflections

Here are my reflections on the work, challenges, and purpose of a Special Agent.

Every day when I put on my jacket bearing the weighty insignia of the Department of Homeland Security, I am reminded of the responsibility my work carries. As an investigator with U.S. Immigration and Customs Enforcement (ICE), my role was as much a calling as it was a career, a daily commitment to upholding the laws that protect our country and its people.

My path to becoming an agent didn't begin with a single defining moment, but rather a deep-seated desire to serve and to seek the truth. Early on, I found myself drawn to the challenge of untangling complex cases, piecing together clues, and fighting for a cause larger than myself. It's not just about following leads, it's about vigilance, intuition, and an enduring belief in the rule of law.

As an agent, my work was varied and seldom predictable. ICE's investigative branch, Homeland Security Investigations (HSI), oversees a wide range of cases, from immigration crimes to transnational criminal activities. My own caseload might include anything from human trafficking and cybercrime to financial fraud and the illegal trade of contraband.

Each day brought a new case, a new challenge, a new chance to make a difference. I spent hours poring over documents, tracing financial transactions, conducting interviews, and collaborating with local, state, and international law enforcement partners.

Surveillance, forensic analysis, and undercover operations were often part of my toolkit. The work was demanding, requiring both patience and agility, and sometimes carried emotional weight, especially in cases involving vulnerable victims.

Balancing Empathy and Duty

One of the misconceptions was that my work was solely about enforcement. In reality, empathy was crucial. I've sat with victims of trafficking who have lost everything, heard their stories, and worked tirelessly to ensure justice for them.

I've also encountered individuals whose circumstances are anything but straightforward, marked by hardship, desperation, and a hope for a better life.

Understanding the human dimension behind every case was essential. We're trained not only to enforce the law, but also to do so with integrity and respect for human dignity. It's a balance between firmness and compassion, and it's what kept me grounded.

Success stemmed from the collaborative efforts of dedicated professionals, including analysts who sift through data, special agents who conduct field operations, and attorneys who prepare cases for prosecution. The network was vast and interconnected. We relied on each other, drawing on diverse skills and perspectives to reach our goals.

On difficult days, it was the sense of camaraderie that motivated me, knowing that each of us played a part in a larger mission.

Ethical Dilemmas

I admit that the work as an agent was physically and emotionally taxing. The cases were often complex and could stretch over months or even years. There were moments when the evidence didn't add up, when leads went cold, or when the outcome wasn't what I'd hoped for.

Ethical dilemmas were part of the territory. We operate under strict guidelines, and every decision must be weighed carefully, not just for its legality, but for its impact on lives. The trust the public places in us was sacred, and I never took that for granted.

Despite the challenges, some moments affirm why I chose this path. I recall the relief in a survivor's eyes after a successful human trafficking operation, the gratitude from communities made safer by dismantling criminal networks, and the rare but precious moments when justice brings closure to those harmed.

Sometimes, my work was quiet and behind the scenes, disrupting the flow of illegal goods, freezing illicit assets, or preventing a crime from happening. These victories may never make headlines, but they shape lives and safeguard communities.

Crime was not static; it evolved in tandem with technological advancements and the flow of information. I was a perpetual student, continually learning new techniques, adapting to changing criminal innovations, and staying ahead of the trends. Regular training, advanced courses, and inter-agency cooperation were fundamental to my success.

I learned to be both skeptical and open-minded, to trust my instincts but always seek corroboration, and to be as relentless as those we pursue.

My personal reflection

If I had to sum up what it meant to be an agent, I would say it's about service, sacrifice, and an unyielding pursuit of truth. It was a job that demanded much but gave back in equal measure, a sense of belonging to something greater, and a daily reminder of the power of integrity.

I knew that each day I walked into my office, I had the chance to make a difference, sometimes small, sometimes profound. That, above all, was why I continued to serve.

The world of a special agent was often painted with sharp strokes of heroism, intrigue, and danger. I believe that popular culture thrives on tales of clandestine operations and daring missions.

Still, beneath the surface, the life of a special agent for me was marked by a tapestry of experiences that shaped not only my career but my very sense of self.

For me, the journey began with a call to serve, an innate desire to protect, to uphold justice, and to contribute to something greater than myself.

The role of a special agent was not chosen lightly; it demanded rigorous training, unwavering commitment, and a willingness to face the unknown. I often reflected on my initial motivations, recalling moments in young adulthood when the seeds of purpose were planted.

Whether inspired by personal experiences or a deep-seated sense of responsibility, the choice to join the ranks was rarely impulsive; it was the culmination of reflection and resolve.

I encountered a world that was far more nuanced than textbooks and simulations could convey. The work was often unpredictable, oscillating between long stretches of surveillance and moments of intense action.

I frequently reflected on the delicate balance between patience and decisiveness, the need for meticulous planning, and the ability to improvise when circumstances change. Every operation, whether routine or extraordinary, became an opportunity for growth, revealing the complexities of human behavior and the challenges of maintaining vigilance in high-stakes environments.

My work was not immune to moral ambiguity. I was frequently faced with ethical dilemmas, forced to make decisions that tested my values and sense of justice.

The drive to do what was right, even when the path was unclear, anchored my actions and shaped my legacy. I still emphasize the importance of accountability, the comfort that comes from procedure, and the necessity of trusting one's instincts.

The demands of the job extended far beyond the office or the field. I often reflect on the personal sacrifices required: time away from family, disrupted routines, and the ever-present possibility of danger.

I remember moments of vulnerability, acknowledging the toll

that stress, uncertainty, and trauma took on me.

I learned to navigate the complexities of balancing duty with personal well-being, recognizing that longevity in the role depends on adaptability and emotional fortitude.

My work was constantly evolving. I reflect on the evolving landscape of threats, including cybercrime, terrorism, and organized crime, alongside the proliferation of new technologies.

Staying ahead required continuous learning, innovation, and collaboration across agencies and borders. The pace of change was daunting, but I embraced the challenge, finding meaning in my ability to adapt and make a positive impact in an ever-evolving world.

Despite the often harsh realities of the job, I discovered that empathy and compassion were vital tools. Whether interviewing witnesses, supporting victims, or negotiating with adversaries, the ability to connect with others on a human level can defuse conflict and build trust. I'm talking about when kindness triumphed over confrontation, when understanding led to resolution, and when my work brought comfort to those in need.

As an agent, I learned to notice what others overlook. The color of a shoelace, the direction a person's eyes flicker when a question is asked, the subtle tremor of a hand, all these become part of a silent language, readable only to those trained to see.

In airports, I sense the difference between nervous fliers and those hiding darker secrets. In crowds, I spot the person who doesn't quite fit, whose gaze is calculating rather than curious.

To me, truth and lies are as distinct as day and night. Over years of interrogations and interviews, I've developed a sixth sense for deceit. Micro-expressions, a fleeting tightening of the jaw, a momentary arch of the brow, betray emotions that words strive to conceal.

The rhythm of speech, the choice of words, the choreography of gestures: all become music to my ears, the melody of truth, the discord of deception.

Yet, I see more than just the lie; I know the motive beneath it. Desperation, fear, greed, or even love each filter into the fabric of a falsehood. This insight is not cynicism, but a hard-earned empathy, a recognition that people rarely lie without reason.

I witnessed both the best and worst of people. I've seen heroism in the selflessness of those who risk all for justice, in the resilience of victims who survive with dignity.

But I also know the cruelty people can inflict: the aftermath of violent crimes, the devastation wrought by betrayal, the cold calculation of organized crime.

Crime scenes become landscapes of memory, each detail a clue, each absence a question. Blood spatter arcs across walls; a photograph sits askew on a mantle; a child's toy, untouched, gathering dust in a corner.

I have documented, analyzed, and sometimes mourned. In the quiet after the chaos, I've carried the weight of what I've seen.

I've seen the multiplicity of identities people possess. Suspects are not mere villains; they are parents, friends, and adversaries all in one. I learned to look for those layers, to see the human beneath the headline, the complexity behind the confession.

Undercover work brought this lesson home. When I assumed a false identity, I saw the world from another's vantage, navigating different moral terrains.

I witnessed firsthand the power of social bonds and the loneliness that deception brings. I saw how easy it was to slip into darkness, and sometimes, how hard it was to return.

I saw grief, hope, and resilience. The faces of families waiting for answers, the fatigue of colleagues after a long operation, the brief flicker of relief when justice was served.

In the end, I saw the world not in black and white, but in an infinite array of shades of gray. Each day brought new mysteries, new challenges, and the enduring hope that what I did made a difference.

CHAPTER 26

Changes in Law Enforcement

Over the past half-century, law enforcement agencies worldwide, particularly in the United States, have undergone significant transformations. Significant shifts in policies, technology, organizational structures, community relationships, and the very philosophy of policing have marked the journey from the 1970s to the present day.

Understanding how law enforcement has evolved provides key insights into broader societal changes and the ongoing challenges faced by police in the modern era.

The 1970s were an essential time in the development of modern policing. Many police departments resembled paramilitary organizations, focusing on a clear hierarchy and strict rules. Back then, policing was primarily focused on responding to crimes after they had occurred, rather than actively working to prevent them from happening.

Technology and Equipment have changed. Police equipment was relatively basic. We relied on radios, handwritten reports, and paper files for communication and record-keeping. Patrol cars were equipped with simple lights and sirens, and forensic technology was in its infancy. Fingerprinting was the gold standard for identification, while DNA evidence was virtually unknown at the time.

Our training focused on physical fitness, firearms usage, and traditional investigative techniques. There was limited training in cultural competence, de-escalation, or crisis intervention.

The relationship we had between the police and the communities was often strained. The concept of "community policing" had not yet been widely embraced.

The 1970s were a time of rising crime rates in larger cities, with urban unrest and fears about drug use and violent crime dominating public discourse. Policing strategies frequently reflected a "tough on crime" approach, including aggressive enforcement of drug laws.

The decades since the 1970s have seen an explosion of technological advancements. The introduction of computers revolutionized record-keeping, dispatch, and communications. Mobile data terminals first appeared in patrol cars in the 1980s, followed by the introduction of body-worn cameras, GPS tracking, and sophisticated surveillance tools in the 2000s and beyond.

Modern officers now have access to real-time data, digital forensics, and rapid information sharing with other agencies.

Today's law enforcement receives significantly more

comprehensive training than their counterparts of the 1970s. Training now encompasses cultural diversity, implicit bias, de-escalation tactics, mental health crisis response, and ethical decision-making. Accreditation standards and ongoing professional development have become the norm.

A defining feature of modern law enforcement is the heightened emphasis on accountability. Civilian review boards, body cameras, and public reporting of use-of-force incidents offer new mechanisms for transparency. Advances in technology also mean that officers' actions are more likely to be recorded by themselves or by bystanders than ever before.

The policy environment has also evolved. The war on drugs of the 1980s and '90s led to harsh sentencing laws and a dramatic increase in incarceration.

In recent years, however, there has been a move towards criminal justice reform, including efforts to reduce mass incarceration, address wrongful convictions (often aided by DNA evidence), and emphasize rehabilitation over punishment.

Diversity and Representation

The demographics of law enforcement have undergone considerable shifts. Police forces are now more diverse, with increased representation of women and minorities. Recruitment efforts and policies, such as affirmative action, have played a significant role in these changes; however, representation and equity continue to be ongoing challenges.

Despite progress, law enforcement continues to face persistent challenges. The proliferation of firearms, the opioid crisis, cybercrime, and domestic terrorism requires new skills and resources. Meanwhile, incidents of excessive force and officer-involved shootings continue to erode public trust in many cities. Calls for defunding or reimagining policing reflect deep divisions about the role and value of police in society.

The evolution of law enforcement from the 1970s to today is a complex narrative of adaptation, innovation, and, at times, controversy.

Police work has become more technologically advanced, professionalized, and accountable, yet it continues to be shaped by shifting public expectations, social challenges, and the enduring quest for justice and safety.

As societies continue to debate and redefine the role of police, the changes that have occurred underscore the importance of flexibility, transparency, and trust in law enforcement's ongoing mission.

CHAPTER 27

Retirement – the Conclusion

I earned a respectable income; however, I have never been motivated by money, as my main goal has always been to build a career in law enforcement.

My work in law enforcement has truly fulfilled all my expectations. Over the years, I've had the privilege of arresting narcotics traffickers, going undercover within criminal groups, rescuing child victims, investigating terrorism, and even meeting some high-ranking dignitaries along the way.

Reflections on Retirement

After 46 years of serving, it is time to conclude an exceptional law enforcement career. This milestone signifies more than just retirement; it embodies a life dedicated to purpose, filled with courage, compassion, challenges, and successes.

As this final chapter begins, it offers a moment for personal reflection and gratitude towards colleagues, family, friends, and the community that has influenced every day of service.

Forty-six years ago, the world was different. The streets, the uniforms, the technology, and even the very notion of public service have all transformed in ways few could have predicted. Yet, at the heart of it all remained the same unshakable sense of duty, the call to protect, to serve, and to uphold the law with integrity.

Walking into the academy as a young recruit, there was a sense of anticipation mingled with uncertainty. There were lessons to be learned and traditions to be honored.

Over the years, those early days provided a foundation: the discipline instilled by early mentors, the camaraderie of fellow cadets, and the first taste of what it meant to wear the badge with pride.

Over nearly fifty years in law enforcement, the profession has faced various challenges and made significant progress. The tools used have undergone significant transformations from radios to smartphones, typewriters to tablets, and notepads to cloud-based databases. Despite these changes, the essence of the job remains centered on the people: both those being served and those serving.

The journey was filled with numerous milestones. It included first late-night patrols, where trust in instincts and training were equally important. Tense times came with emergencies, rescues, and investigations demanding complete focus and resilience. Yet, there were also moments of profound joy, reunions, family gratitude, and laughter shared in the squad room after tough shifts.

Over time, leadership emerged, along with the responsibility to mentor the next generation of agents. Guiding young recruits, sharing stories and wisdom, and witnessing their growth into confident community protectors became a great source of pride. Each year, the understanding of justice deepened, along with the appreciation of its complexities and responsibilities.

Some memories are as vivid as the day they happened. Law enforcement is not a path for the faint of heart. It has demanded sacrifice, time away from family, sleepless nights, and the weight of decisions that linger long after the shift ends.

But it has also offered wonders. The badge has been both a shield and a beacon, a reminder of the trust bestowed and the promise to never take it for granted.

I didn't serve alone. I have had the support of my family, which has been the quiet strength behind every one of my accomplishments. The patience of a partner who understood the odd hours, the encouragement of a child who grew up with the realities of the job, and the steadfast presence of friends who listened and cared - these relationships have been the anchor through all the turbulence.

My colleagues became more than coworkers; in many ways, they became family. The bonds forged in moments of adversity and joy have lasted through the years. Together, countless officers built a legacy of service, one call, one act of kindness, one intervention at a time.

The decision to retire, even after so many years, was a bittersweet one. There was a sense of loss, leaving behind routines, responsibilities, and the camaraderie of the office. There was also excitement for what comes next. The last shift was not an end, but a new beginning.

Packing up the office, turning in the badge and radio, and walking out for the final time are acts steeped in emotion. There was pride in a job well done, sorrow for the moments that could not be changed, and hope for the future.

Retirement does not erase the legacy left behind. The lessons learned, the lives touched, and the difference made will endure. The transition was an opportunity to rediscover passions set aside, spend cherished time with loved ones, travel, volunteer, or rest in the peace earned over decades of service.

Retirement isn't a loss of identity but a new chapter. The future remains unexplored, offering peace, fulfillment, and treasured memories. The journey continues, just in a different form.

As the last chapter draws to a close, gratitude fills the heart. Thank you to every colleague, friend, and family member who helped make this journey possible. Thank you to the community for the privilege of serving, protecting, and being part of it.

Forty-six years in law enforcement was a remarkable journey. As this chapter ends and the next begins, there is comfort in knowing that the values of courage, integrity, and compassion will carry forward, not just in one life, but in all those touched along the way.

I will miss the camaraderie, the adrenaline of a case coming together, and the satisfaction of seeing justice served. There will be moments of longing, sudden flashes of nostalgia for the rhythms of duty. Yet, there is also a sense of peace, a readiness to embrace what lies ahead.

My Prayer

After forty-six years of service in law enforcement, I am embarking on a new chapter in my life.

Lord, You have watched over me since my early days as a police officer and through my years as a federal agent. During all the long nights, uncertain calls, dangerous moments, and the quiet hours of service unseen by many, You were there.

I sincerely appreciate the calling You placed on my life, a calling to serve and protect, to pursue justice and mercy, and to face the unknown each day with courage and faith.

For forty-six years, You have been my shield and strength. You've guided my steps, steadied my hand, and calmed my heart during times when fear threatened to take over. You've whispered hope when shadows grew longer, and You've celebrated every act of kindness, every life touched, and every wrong made right.

Lord, I made many sacrifices, missed many holidays, and took risks on behalf of strangers, carrying their burdens quietly so that others could sleep in safety. You alone know the depths of the weight I bore, the decisions made in split seconds, the scars both seen and unseen. Thank You for being my constant companion, for walking beside me through every trial and triumph.

As I lay down the badge I have worn with honor, please grant me the peace that surpasses all understanding. Fill my days with the assurance that my work mattered, that my legacy will continue in the lives I've protected.

Grant me also the grace of forgiveness for myself and for others. Where regrets linger or wounds remain, bring healing and wholeness. Where memories bring pain, bring Your Spirit. Restore my soul, O Lord, and renew my strength for the days ahead.

As I begin this new chapter of life, I pray for Your continued guidance and blessing. May retirement not be a conclusion, but the start of new adventures, deeper connections, and great joy. Open doors to new ways of serving and loving others, whether through small acts of kindness or roles only You can envision.

I pray for all law enforcement personnel still serving. May my legacy serve as a guiding light, inspiring others to act with integrity, compassion, and humility. Protect those on the thin blue line, bestow them with wisdom and courage, and draw them nearer to You.

After forty-six years of faithful service, I retired not only with gratitude but also with the deep and abiding love of our Creator.

In the name of Jesus Christ, my Lord and Savior,

Amen.